UNCHAINED WEALTH

HOW TO BECOME FINANCIALLY FREE IN YOUR 20S
YOUR ROADMAP TO PASSIVE INCOME

MICHAEL LANCTOT

ISBN: 979-8-9896477-0-5

Book Design by HMDPUBLISHING

Important Disclaimer

The content in this book is intended solely for educational and entertainment purposes. It is not a substitute for professional advice and should not be interpreted as such. The information presented herein does not replace the personalized guidance and advice of a qualified financial advisor, investment consultant, or attorney.

The author and publisher expressly disclaim all liability and responsibility for any loss, damage, or adverse outcomes that may arise, either directly or indirectly, from the application or misinterpretation of the information contained within this book. This includes, but is not limited to, any consequential damages, financial losses, or legal implications.

Because individual circumstances can differ widely, the strategies and recommendations presented in this book may not be suitable for your specific situation. Before making any legal or financial decisions, it is strongly recommended that you consult with qualified professionals to address your unique needs and concerns.

Proceed with this understanding.

"Success is something you attract by the person you become."
—Jim Rohn

CONTENTS

ROCK BOTTOM TO MILLIONAIRE

Look, I get it. I've been exactly where you are—financially broke in my 20s.

At 22 years old, I hit financial rock bottom, staring at what felt like a dead end. Bankruptcy wasn't just knocking at my door; it had its foot wedged in. But you know what? Three years later, I was a millionaire. How's that for a turnaround? I didn't hit the lottery or inherit a fortune. I earned it through blood, sweat, tears, and passive income.

Now, before you roll your eyes at another rags-to-riches story, hear me out. The incredible thing about where I'm at now isn't just the bank account; it's the knowledge and experience I've gained. If I lost every penny tomorrow, I wouldn't be back to square one. Why? Because I know how to build it all over again.

So, why am I telling you all this? Because this book you're holding is not just paper and ink. It's a roadmap—a direct route that I've paved through trial and error just so you can avoid the detours and roadblocks and get a head start on your finances.

You might feel trapped by your financial circumstances now, but I promise you, there's a way out. I've kicked down the door to financial freedom, and I'm holding it open for you. All you need to do is walk through and follow in my footsteps.

But here's the catch: you've got to be all in. Don't just skim through this book like it's a beach read. Devour it. Make notes. Challenge yourself. The path to financial independence isn't a lazy river; it's a turbulent rapid, and you're going to need every strategy in these pages to navigate it.

Lastly, enough with being reckless—whether it's your time or your money. Every second you waste and every penny you mismanage is a missed opportunity for growth. So grab a highlighter, mark up these pages, and get ready to level up your life.

Are you still with me? Fantastic. Let's light that fire in your belly and get you on the fast track to a life most people only dream of.

Are you ready to change your stars? Then let's get to it!

To Your Future Success,

Mike Lanctot

CHAPTER 1
THE PARADOX

"A formal education will make you a living;
self-education will make you a fortune."
— Jim Rohn

"You need to work harder; your generation is the laziest group ever. When I was your age, I worked four jobs, ate once daily, and only slept for 2 hours between my shifts."

Sound familiar?

Oh, the wisdom of the ages, or so they'd like us to believe. Previous generations loved to blame our financial struggles on a supposed lack of work ethic. But let's get real – we're dealing with the worst inflation ever, stagnant wages, skyrocketing costs of college, food, housing, and pretty much everything else essential for daily life (computer, cell phone, Wi-Fi, a reliable car, you name it) is getting more expensive.

The harsh truth? We're in a worse financial place than our previous generations, but — and it's a big but — there's also more opportunity now than ever. And what's with all the sage advice from parents, grandparents, and friends urging us to follow in their footsteps? Do the same old, same old, and expect different results? It's madness.

Yet, here's the kicker: More people are becoming financially free now than ever. So, how on earth are people getting ahead in this financial whirlpool? What's their secret? What did they do differently?

Our minds and bodies are at peak performance when we're young, but we are told to waste our youth being reckless. Have fun while young, they say. Go to college, rack up debt, get a car with even more debt, rent an apartment (because who doesn't love throwing money at someone else?), and take up hobbies that drain time and money. If that's the recipe for success, then something's seriously wrong.

That advice ends right here and right now. From this point forward, I'm going to twirl your brain, upgrade your thinking, and get down to the brass tacks of financial freedom. It's time to define what freedom means to you, quantify it, identify the trap you're in, and break free. We'll talk about how to own a business you can afford, how to develop multiple income streams, the allure of passive income, and how it all ties to freedom.

And here's the beautiful Paradox: While it's more challenging than ever to navigate the financial landscapes, it's this very environment that's forging new opportunities and pathways to success. The conventional wisdom of the past no longer holds; instead, the doors are open to innovative thinking, disruptive strategies, and the courage to break free from the constraints that held previous generations. Embrace the paradox, take the reins of your financial destiny, and never let the judgments of the past define your future. Success in today's world doesn't come from following the well-trodden path but from carving out your unique journey, guided by resilience, creativity, and the willingness to redefine what's possible.

So, buckle up because if you want to make it in today's world, you'll need to get uncomfortable and scrappy—and that means no blaming, no being a victim, and no complaining; just good 'old-fashioned being focused and working smart.

But hey, you wouldn't be here if you weren't up for the challenge, right?

CHAPTER 2
BECOMING FINANCIALLY FREE

"Don't live the same day over and over again and call that a life. Life is about evolving mentally, spiritually, and emotionally."
— **Germany Kent**

Becoming financially Free — doesn't that sound on point?

But here's the thing: It's not about status—putting on airs, driving a G-Wagon, or pretending to be something you're not. It's about digging deep into yourself and realizing that wealth creation isn't reserved for the elite few. Nope, it's for anyone willing to change their mindset, develop the right habits, and do the work. Are you ready to buy in?

So, you've been scrolling through social media and seeing all the other young influencers living your dream in their 20s. You want what they have but don't know what to do. That's the point: success is not about doing; it's about becoming. You have to become the person with the awareness, thinking, and habits to create that mountain of success. To do that, you have to become financially fearless. You have to break through the traps and non-truths and learn the strategies that will get you on the right course to becoming wealthy. Because, let's face it, life's too short to be building someone else's dream or stuck in someone else's game. It's time to create your own rules and your own success.

First, let's get clear about the four degrees of financial freedom that serve as critical benchmarks on your path to becoming financially fearless.

- Financially Set: Your income exceeds your expenses, and you are comfortable.

- Financially Free: Your passive income exceeds your expenses.

- Financially Secure: Your passive income is diversified enough that you would be set if your main income source took a hit.

- Financially Fearless: Your passive income greatly exceeds your expenses, so you have time and resources to pour into business ventures.

These aren't just catchy terms; they're meaningful benchmarks that help you gauge where you're at and what you've got to focus on next. It's like having a financial GPS, guiding you from 'Financially Set' to the ultimate destination of being 'Financially Fearless.' But knowing the route isn't enough—you also need some on-the-ground experience to make it all real. That's why we're shifting our focus to Tony. His simple story is a perfect example of the tension between ambition and reality—between what you aim for and what you're currently capable of.

⸻⧂⧂⧂⸻

Tony is a natural-born leader. He has excelled in everything he's done, and his image is built around being known for his consistent, unwavering success. Tony plays college baseball and has an aptitude for entrepreneurship. He's done sales in the past and has realized the financial success that can come from an influx of cash.

Coincidentally, as he was planning his summer, he received a message about a sales position with a pest control company. He did some research, met with his parents, and realized this was exactly what he wanted to get into to start his sales and entrepreneurship journey. Day one was very different than he was expecting. People weren't rushing to buy from him; he was doing the work, but people weren't pulling out their credit cards.

After three days had passed, Tony decided he needed to focus on baseball and weightlifting, and there was no way he could work this schedule and stay in baseball shape. After his manager talked him through it and made a plan to do his workouts and work pest control, he admitted what was really going on. He hated not being good at sales and couldn't stand it anymore. He would rather quit and not deal with the rejection than push through and gain a new skill.

Tony's story happens all the time. People want the result but don't want to bend their minds to become the person who gets the results. Financial success won't come easy, and it won't come to those who aren't okay with pushing through the discomfort. Take, for example, Joseph Sanchez. He grew up in foster care and had a tough time at school since he was skinnier and awkward and would get picked on constantly. No matter what, though, he wanted out of his current situation. He worked multiple jobs, and in one instance, when he was delivering sandwiches to a sales company that was tabling at a campus, he looked at their opportunity and took it. Sales didn't come naturally, and the rejection stung. However, Joseph focused on what he could become, unlike Tony, and didn't let the discomfort get to him.

To craft a fearless financial mindset, the most important thing you can do is focus on developing new skills and ways to put your money to work for you. You cannot succeed today without the discipline of being bad at something until you're good at it and doing it until it's on repeat. Things are changing too fast. Nobody knows what the next invention will be that will put your job at risk. Will there be a new career or opportunity that is the next gold rush? Of course, there will be— we've seen that for the last 40 years. Skill development is the most important thing you can pursue to insulate yourself from the ever-changing financial tides—especially early on when starting your career. The more you can do, the more you know, and the more you can relate to other people, the more successful you will be.

⸙

Starting early in high school, I never held a job for more than two years. When I started working at a pizza shop, I quit once I learned how to make pizza and sandwiches and became one of the best. I also worked as a delivery man and quit once I became great and efficient. When I started working in a lab and figured out how to collect data, compartmentalize, and learn the skills that benefited me from that experience, I quit. I have never worked anywhere for more than two years.

When I was working for my first pest control company, I quit after becoming a top recruiter and one of the best salesmen in the office. When I worked for Edge and became one of the top managers, someone running one of the top offices, I quit. I never desired to be just at the top. I needed to be among the top producers, and once I reached the top and found a plateau of development where they could no longer continue to help me scale my skills, I left.

At some point, you have to make a decision. Do you want to plateau and be comfortable, or do you want to go on and create more? In one of his books, Robert Kiyosaki wrote that even though he was financially stable, he went into the military to become a pilot. Why? He wanted to gain the skill to be a pilot to do more with his life.

Embracing this truth is central to your journey toward financial literacy, financial freedom, and continuous skill development. Growth must be rapid and unceasing. If you find yourself stagnant, it's time for a tough conversation with yourself and the people you work with, and perhaps a new path is the next logical step.

Sometimes, working for others to acquire new skills is the smart choice. Imagine an opportunity to learn from the best Audi dealer mechanics in the world, absorbing intricate details of the trade instead of fumbling around as a mediocre mechanic. This learning experience can be far more valuable than going solo, even if it means a temporary pay cut. Once those refined skills become yours, it's time to move on, always aiming for new heights and fresh opportunities.

Through the relentless pursuit of knowledge, coupled with the metaphorical calluses you accumulate from change and discomfort, you can create a path to push through the barrier of entry. You embark on a journey to financial freedom, a path lined with opportunities and empowerment.

But this journey isn't just about ambition and resilience; it requires financial smarts. Here's a money skill that will pay dividends in the long run:

Pay attention to making the best use of your money. Every time you spend, ask yourself, "How is this going to earn me money?" or "How can I capitalize on this?" Consider your expenses—whether fixed, like rent, mortgage, car payments, insurance, utilities, and food, or variable, like entertainment and luxury items—as opportunities, not mere costs.

Education, too, can be either a fixed or non-fixed expense, depending on your circumstances. Traditional financial wisdom might tell you to cut non-fixed expenses and wait 40-50 years to retire. But who wants to live a life confined by a constant fear of spending money, so focused on cutting costs that life becomes colorless and dull?

I once saw an episode of TLC with a woman who was so "frugal" that she spent less than 12 dollars a week on basic necessities. Her methods were extreme, to say the least: cooking dinner in the dishwasher. Scraping leftovers back into containers. Using one light bulb for the entire house. Who wants to live like that? It's a grim existence. There is a better way to embrace life's pleasures without financial recklessness.

Becoming financially free hinges on your ability to acquire valuable skills and effectively market them. Let's dive deeper into this concept with some additional details and examples.

First and foremost, identifying skills with economic value is crucial. Think about individuals who excel in sales, like the top-notch salesman who consistently closes deals and generates revenue for their company. Or consider someone who's mastered the art of flipping cars—turning neglected vehicles into profitable assets. Perhaps you're a master when it comes to playing the saxophone. When recognized for their marketability, all these skills can pave the way to financial freedom.

Now, let's look at how these skills can propel you forward and strengthen your financial foundation. A top-notch salesman, for instance, can leverage their persuasive abilities to boost their income through commissions and bonuses. The car-flipping expert can turn their passion into a thriving business, buying and selling vehicles for a profit. As for the saxophonist, opportunities like teaching, performing, or recording can turn their talent into a lucrative venture. Better yet, develop a niche training program on YouTube that you can monetize.

But don't underestimate the skills you might be overlooking. That seemingly simple pizza-making hobby you enjoy on weekends could have untapped potential. Imagine turning it into a YouTube channel where you share your pizza-making expertise, attracting viewers, and potentially monetizing your passion through sponsorships and ads. The key here is always keeping an eye on your skills and using them intentionally.

Financial freedom is achieved by recognizing the economic value of your skills and harnessing them to boost your income and fortify your financial standing. And remember, even the skills you least expect could hold untapped potential, so be open to creative ways of leveraging them to your advantage.

CHALLENGE |
BECOMING FINANCIALLY FREE

Analyze Your Mastery

1. Reflect on what you've mastered. What are you excellent at? Take pride in these abilities.

2. Consider what sparks your interest. What's calling you? Identify where you want to grow and explore.

3. Set the stage for what comes next. Your current expertise and future desires are your roadmap to success.

4. Marketing Potential: Harnessing Your Skills.

5. Determine the commercial value of your skills. What can you market based on what you've mastered and what you want to pursue?

6. Look for unexpected business opportunities or career shifts based on your unique skill set.

7. Align your skills with opportunities to create value and expand. It's about more than just money; it's about carving out your unique path.

8. Reflect on these insights and explore them thoroughly. They are your guiding stars on the journey to success.

CHAPTER 3
OUTSMARTING THE FINANCIAL TRAP

"Financial freedom is available to those who learn about it and work for it."
— **Robert Kiyosaki**

Are you comfortably numb, feeling stuck in a financial rut, and chained to old ways of thinking but not knowing how to get out? Do you want more out of life? More money, more time, more freedom, more lifestyle?

Here's what's going wrong for so many people: They're caught in outdated thinking, holding onto the belief that the path our parents and grandparents followed was the only road to financial freedom. They're clinging to a script that's been handed down for generations without realizing that the rules have changed, and so have the opportunities.

Picture this: a world where you're not confined to a traditional 9-5 grind, trading hours for a paycheck, and watching your dreams gather dust on a shelf. Imagine breaking free from the shackles of conventional employment, whether you're locked into a salaried job or hustling as a 1099 worker. And yes, even if you're a business owner struggling to balance the demands of ownership with the elusive promise of freedom, It's time to transform from merely owning a job to building a life you love.

The good news is that more people are becoming millionaires than ever before, and it's not because they stumbled upon a pot of gold or won the lottery. It's because they developed a wealth-creation mindset. They broke free from traditional thinking, grabbed onto the coattails of mentors, and embraced opportunities.

So, where are you in the grand scheme of finances? Are you ensnared in the "glorious" trap of financial stagnation and ready to level up, or are you still resisting the growth you need to go through to play a bigger game with your life? If you're resisting, then reading this book is a waste of your time, so you might as well put it down and shelf it until you become teachable. But if you're ready to level up, Then, it's time for a full-court press to elevate your mindset.

The "glorious trap" emerged from the ashes of history, a relic of the Great Depression and the seismic shifts brought about by the Industrial Revolution. In those transformative times, many people migrated from traditional rural farms to the highly energized epicenter of the Industrial Revolution—major cities across the county. They longed for job security, benefits, and the promise of a steady paycheck. And thus, the "glorious trap" was born.

Fast forward to today, and here we are, still feeling the echoes of the industrial revolution resonating in the corridors of our collective mindset. It's the place where employees are dutifully punching the clock, trading their precious hours for a paycheck, as if time itself were a commodity you could buy at the store. And what do they get in return? The thrilling promise of benefits in exchange for the soul-crushing monotony of a predictable paycheck

It's not just our 9-to-5 warriors feeling the tug of this ancient mindset. Now we've got a whole brigade of 1099 workers—the freelancers and gig economy daredevils. These people are like modern-day treasure hunters, forever chasing the next gig fix to keep their financial equilibrium from going belly-up. It's a relentless cycle, a bit like a dog chasing its own tail—excited for its next treat, but with invoices and coffee shop meetings instead of bones and table scraps.

The Industrial Revolution left a lasting mark, and it's up to you to find the sweet spot between breaking free from a regular paycheck and the wild freedom that comes from creating your own stream of financial wealth.

Even business owners, those who dared to step outside the employee mold, can find themselves ensnared in the trap. They might have taken the leap into entrepreneurship to escape the shackles of employment, only to discover that their business has transformed into yet another job – one they own but can't escape. The dream of calling the shots and steering their destiny has often metamorphosed into a relentless grind, an unending series of tasks and obligations that leaves little room for the freedom they envisioned.

It's a classic narrative, the "glorious trap," where the promises of financial security, stability, and societal acceptance intertwine with the shackles of conformity, monotony, and limited growth. It's a place where time becomes a commodity to be traded, and dreams quietly wither away, suffocated by the weight of routine. This trap, a paradoxical fusion of aspiration and stagnation, is where both time and financial freedom often go to languish, a silent sacrifice made on the altar of outdated norms.

But beyond this narrative of entrapment, an alternative path to financial freedom hides—the path of accumulating assets and setting up multiple streams of passive income. If this intrigues you, if you are ready to jump ship on old thinking, then it's time to rewrite the rules, reimagine your trajectory, and reshape your relationship with time and money. After all, life is too short to be ensnared in the antiquated thinking of yesterday. Let's forge a new path toward your definition of success, where freedom and prosperity are not opposing forces but partners in an extraordinary life.

Let me be bold and say that if you're stuck in this trap, it's because of one of two reasons—you're either stupid or lazy. Harsh, but let's dig into it. Don't go throwing this book across the room just yet; hear me out. If you're stupid, don't take it personally. I was there, too. Our entire public education system teaches us to fail. We're not taught to think for ourselves but instead to conform to a narrative and be employees, not business owners, entrepreneurs, or investors.

Consider this: From the very moment we step into the world of education, we're funneled into a system that's all about conformity and rewards for following the rules. Think about those classroom days – they're more about training us to be efficient employees, not exactly helping us become innovative thinkers or savvy entrepreneurs. We're told to stand in line, follow instructions, memorize information, and aim for those top grades—skills that could make us experts at following someone else's lead but don't quite equip us for crafting our own unique path through life.

As we journey through the academic years, we get really good at acing standardized tests, stuffing our heads with facts, and fitting perfectly into the molds that society has carefully shaped for us. Financial literacy, entrepreneurship, or investing? They rarely even make it into the conversation. Instead, the system seems to push us towards the promise of a safe job, the comfort of a steady routine, and the allure of job benefits—the very things that contribute to what I like to call the "glorious trap."

It's like we're served the notion on a silver platter that success comes from climbing that corporate ladder, sticking to the safe routes, and following that straight path everyone's talking about. In this story, it's almost like our value is measured by how well we can excel in someone else's game, not by our ability to come up with new ideas, create our own opportunities, and shape our destiny.

But here's the hook. That story is outdated and doesn't tell the whole truth. The world is different now, and success isn't just a one-size-fits-all concept. The game has changed, and the tools to break free from the "glorious trap" and achieve financial freedom are actually within reach. It's time we questioned the norm, pushed back against the traditional education mold, and embraced a fresh mindset and set of strategies that can help us thrive beyond the confines of that old trap.

From this point forward, think of the remainder of this book as your compass, showing you the ways to navigate this new landscape, break the chains of old-school thinking, and rewrite your story on your own terms. It's your chance to reclaim control over your own path, redefine what success means to you, and set off on a journey towards financial abundance, personal fulfillment, and discovering your true potential.

If you're leaning towards the lazy side of the spectrum, well, I'd advise you to steer clear of any books by the likes of David Goggins or Grant Cardone because you will not relate to their relentless mindset. Seriously, don't even think about picking up their stuff. Instead, just go ahead and settle yourself onto that trusty couch of yours, queue up some motivational videos—after you're done reading this book, of course—and let's start the process of waving that sluggish, couch-dwelling version of yourself goodbye. It's all about taking that action.

Now, let's dive even deeper into this trap and uncover why it's got such a tight grip on our lives. We're living in the age of smartphones and endless information, where everything we need is just a tap away. You'd think with all this knowledge and convenience, we'd all be crushing it, right? I mean, skill-building, hustling on our own terms, and chasing our creative dreams – it's all right there at our fingertips. But the reality isn't always as straightforward.

Now, here's the twist: the trap's ultimate weapon? It's called financial illiteracy, and it's like this fog that blurs our vision of what's possible. Most of us tend to stick to the traditional 9-to-5 grind and the routines we're used to rather than diving into new opportunities that could totally shake things up. And it makes sense. That's what we've been told is the safe path.

But there's more to the financial illiteracy story. After high school, a lot of people barely ever touch books, let alone ones that could help them navigate the complex world of finances. If you haven't developed a habit of reading books that improve your skills and awareness, then you are keeping yourself caught in a loop of wanting more but setting your own trap. But you don't have to stay stuck in that cycle. Financial literacy is your ticket out. If you're scratching your head wondering what that even means, don't worry – you're not alone because it is not taught in schools, but it definitely should be a top priority.

Financial literacy is like having superpowers that equip you with the skills to make smart choices about money. It's knowing how to invest, buy assets, start companies, understand the financial jargon, and basically rule the world of finance like a boss. With financial literacy in your toolkit, you'll be ready to tackle the world, make savvy choices, and carve out a path to financial success that's truly your own.

The trap we're talking about isn't just about financial literacy; it's also an awareness trap that keeps people from expanding their minds and skills. It's like a sneaky snare that makes you think you've got it all figured out and that there's no more room to learn. But let's get real here – who wants to be stuck in a narrow mindset, missing out on all the amazing ideas and opportunities out there? Not us, that's for sure.

So, here's the deal—if you're in the game of door-to-door sales, you've seen it all too often. People hit the summer hard, making banks feel like there's no tomorrow. But then what happens? The rest of the year rolls around, and they're left scratching their heads, wondering where it all went. It's like they're on a roller coaster ride of income and expenses, and they've got no control over the wheel.

Pest control, solar sales—you name it, the story's the same. It's their golden season, and they rake in the cash. But what happens next is a different story altogether. Instead of investing wisely or building a solid foundation, they go on a spending spree. They inflate their expenses, burden themselves with liabilities, and throw money at things that don't even make sense in the long run.

What's the takeaway here? It's all about that hustle attitude. Don't just wait around for opportunities to knock on your door; go out there and create them. Don't fall for the allure of easy gains only to lose it all in the blink of an eye with reckless spending. Instead, hustle smart, learn from the trap's lessons, and pave your way to financial stability and success. Let's not be the ones who fall for the easy cheese on the mouse trap—we're better than that.

Meet Travis, a guy who had his own store and managed to rake in a substantial income, somewhere between $400,000 and $450,000. Sounds impressive, right? But here's the problem: When we took a closer look at Travis's financial situation, we discovered a rather unsettling truth. Despite his considerable earnings, he had nothing to show for it in terms of assets. In fact, he found himself staring down a hefty tax bill due to his spending spree on non-deductible expenses. Imagine that! He took his entire family on a European vacation, splurged on various purchases that didn't contribute to his financial well-being, and ended up in a financial bind.

Travis's tale isn't unique; it's a familiar storyline for many 1099 workers and business owners. It's not just about how much money you're bringing in or how much you're not bringing in either. The trap's essence lies in complacency and stagnation. It's the feeling of being stuck, neither progressing nor improving.

Travis fell into this pitfall because he got comfortable with his earnings. He stopped striving for more, and instead, he let it all slip away, leading him to an unfavorable financial situation. Unfortunately, Travis's situation is more common than you'd think. Many people become complacent, allowing their expenses to balloon and, ultimately, finding themselves in a similar predicament.

The key to avoiding this financial trap lies in one word: progress. As your income increases, the gap between your earnings and your expenses should widen. That's the secret sauce to sidestep the trap. You have to keep moving forward, making sure your income outpaces the growth in your expenses.

But here's the reality check: If your expenses and income are growing at the same pace, or worse, if your expenses are outpacing your income, you're in DEFCON emergency mode. Imagine you're that mouse caught in a trap, peanut butter in sight, and the bar about to snap down on you. That's where you are right now. It's a critical situation that demands immediate action.

Now, let's talk about those four stages of the trap:

Stage One

At this stage, your expenses and income are either rising at the same rate or your expenses are going up faster. You might be feeling a pinch, but perhaps justify the situation by thinking it's just a phase.

Maybe you got a pay raise, but your rent went up too. Or perhaps you've adopted some new habits—like dining out more often or joining a high-end gym—that are quickly consuming your extra cash. This is the warning stage, where it's crucial to start re-evaluating your spending habits before they spiral out of control.

Stage Two

Here, your expenses are gradually increasing and threatening to catch up with your income. You're still in the safe zone, but the margin is thinning out. It's like walking on a tightrope. Maybe you've had a few unexpected medical bills or car repairs. Your monthly subscription services have started adding up, and you find that you're dipping into your savings more often than you'd like. You're not in immediate danger, but the alarm bells are definitely starting to ring. It's a call to action, reminding you to revise your budget or find additional streams of income.

Stage Three

At this stage, both your expenses and income are going up, but things are starting to feel tight. You're managing, but barely. Perhaps your promotion came with a better paycheck but also higher expectations and stress, leading you to indulge in retail therapy or frequent vacations to unwind. Simultaneously, you may have had life changes like a new baby or a move to a pricier area that have elevated your monthly outgoings. You're still afloat, but the water level is uncomfortably close to the edge of the boat. Your financial resilience is dwindling, and you know that a significant setback could tip the scales.

Stage Four

Expenses have overtaken income, causing extreme financial strain and potentially leading to life-altering decisions like bankruptcy or divorce. This is the point of no return, where daily life becomes an unbearable struggle. You're working non-stop, barely sleeping or eating, and juggling multiple jobs to make ends meet. Arguments with your spouse about finances and potential divorce loom because your financial situation is so dire. Fixed expenses have locked you in, and it seems impossible to escape. It's like being trapped in a maze with no way out. You can't get out of lease agreements.

Let me tell you about Cory, a guy who spearheaded a sales career with dreams of financial success and all the possibilities it could unlock. After just a few summers, Cory quickly climbed the ranks and emerged as a top producer, bringing in over $100,000 each season. Year after year, his earnings grew, and he felt himself improving. As life progressed, so did his expenses. Marriage, kids, lavish trips, and various indulgences for his family meant that, despite his growing income, he always found himself saying, "This year is the year" for saving.

But here's the plot twist: Every time he thought he was on the cusp of saving, something unexpected cropped up, draining his accounts yet again. Five years into his career, Cory made a bold move. He purchased a duplex, listed it on Airbnb, and envisioned a future of passive income. His plan? Save up for the next investment. However, time marched on, and another five years slipped by without him adding to his real estate portfolio. Despite making a solid income—between $100,000 and $300,000 annually for a decade—Cory surveyed his life and realized he owned just one duplex and a collection of trinkets.

So, where did the over $1.5 million he earned disappear? It's a head-scratcher. The culture feeds us a lie: the solution to our discontent is to earn more money, and all our financial issues will vanish. But here's the catch: too many people raise their income while simultaneously amplifying their problems. They take fancier vacations, upgrade their cars, buy a bigger house, and now they're tethered to their higher earnings. If that income wavers, they teeter on the brink of financial ruin because they financed their entire lifestyle.

This deceitful notion is the ultimate trap we've unknowingly fallen into. We're toiling harder, producing more to achieve a better life, yet all the while, we're digging ourselves into a deeper abyss. The first step toward resolution is awareness.

Think about it: for the next three to four decades, you're working for someone else's success. That's mind-boggling. Day by day, you'll struggle to make ends meet, make sacrifices, and compromise on providing the life you wish for your family. Meanwhile, you're pouring your sweat into the success of another entity. This trap isn't exclusive to any income bracket; it ensnares people from all walks of life in one form or another. But don't get discouraged. Acknowledging being caught in this trap is the first step toward breaking free. Your hard work should fuel your dreams, not somebody else's. Let's break free from this trap and build the life we genuinely want.

CHALLENGE |
OUTSMARTING THE FINANCIAL TRAP

1. **Identify Your Current Stage:** Take a moment to reflect on which stage of the financial trap you currently find yourself in. Are you at Stage One, where expenses and income are growing at the same rate or expenses are outpacing income? Are you at Stage Two, where expenses are beginning to creep up and compete with your income? Maybe you're at Stage Three, where balancing your increasing expenses and income is becoming tough, or perhaps you've reached Stage Four, where expenses have overtaken income, leading to significant financial strain.

2. **Seek Inspiration from Escapers:** Research and find people who have successfully escaped the financial trap. What actions did they take to break free? Did they focus on marketing their skills or maintaining low expenses? Analyze their journey and learn from their strategies.

3. **Calculate Your Income-Expense Ratio:** Calculate your current income-to-expense ratio. Divide your total income by your monthly expenses to determine where you stand. This ratio will give you an idea of how well you're managing your financial situation.

4. **Five Ways to Increase Your Income:** Brainstorm five actionable ways to increase your income. These could involve leverag-

ing your skills, exploring side hustles, or seeking new opportunities. Think creatively about how you can boost your earnings.

5. **Five Ways to Decrease Your Expenses:** List five practical ways you can trim down your expenses. Consider areas where you can cut unnecessary costs or make smarter choices. These small changes can add up over time.

6. **Create a One-Week Action Plan:** Put together a timeline for the upcoming week to implement the changes you've identified. Assign specific dates to each task, whether it's pursuing income-boosting opportunities or reducing your expenses. This step-by-step plan will help you stay organized and committed to your goals.

By engaging in these end-of-chapter exercises, you'll be actively taking steps toward understanding your current financial situation, learning from successful people, and creating a practical action plan to escape the financial trap. Remember, progress requires action, and with these exercises, you're setting yourself on a path toward a more financially empowered future.

CHAPTER 4

THE FOUR FINANCIAL SCENARIOS

"Before you can become a millionaire, you must learn to think like one. You must learn how to motivate yourself to counter fear with courage."
—Thomas J. Stanley

L et's dive deeper into the complex universe of personal finance, exploring it as if it were a 4x4 grid where your income and credit-worthiness define your position. Think of it like a financial football field, where your offense is your income and your defense is your credit strategy.

Depending on how well you play in both arenas, you can find yourself in one of four distinctive quadrants. These quadrants serve as a snapshot of your current financial health, a mirror reflecting both your triumphs and your areas for improvement. The goal? To understand where you currently stand and plot the best route to becoming the MVP in your own financial game. So, which quadrant do you find yourself in today?

1. **High-Income, High Credit:** These are the financial quarterbacks, throwing touchdowns in both income and credit management. They're the team captains of the money game.

2. **High-Income, Low Credit:** You're making a killing in the earnings department, but your credit game needs some coaching. It's like having a fast car but fumbling with the gears.

3. **Low-Income, High Credit:** Your income might not be MVP-level, but you're hitting all your free throws when it comes to credit. Think of it as being a skilled sniper on the financial battlefield.

4. **Low-Income, Low Credit:** You're in the trenches—money's tight, and credit's a struggle. It's like going into battle with just a pocket knife.

High Income High Credit	High Income Low Credit
Low Income High Credit	Low Income Low Credit

When I say "Low Credit," I'm not referring solely to your credit score. It's more about your credit strategy and how you navigate the twists and turns of the credit world. Think of it as a strategic game where knowing when to play your cards can make all the difference.

Now, let's put faces in these quadrants. Picture a freshly minted doctor stepping out of the medical battlefield – that's a classic scenario of high-income, low credit. They're earning a lot, but student loans are riding shotgun.

On the flip side, imagine a 25-year-old mechanic who's got their financial game on lock – that's the essence of low-income high credit. They're keeping their financial ship steady, skillfully managing payments, and making every dollar count.

Of course, there are exceptions, but aligning with the broader trend is wiser. Your goal is to sync up with the majority, not the outliers. While your circumstances might be unique, being prepared for the norm is a better strategy than being caught off guard. Different professions often correspond with specific quadrants, adding an intriguing layer to your financial exploration. It's time to unveil your money quadrant and improve your financial game!

Let's explore the four financial corners – where are you right now, and where do you want to be?

Quadrant 1: High Income, High Credit

This mirrors the classic "American Dream" scenario we all envision – lavish homes, stylish cars, exclusive club memberships, and cherished annual vacations if you're situated here. Fantastic! This is the pinnacle most strive for.

Odds are, you're well off due to sound financial choices or a sprinkle of good fortune. But here's the twist: the illusion of being in Quadrant 1 when you might actually be in Quadrant 2 is real. Escaping the clutches of Quadrant 2 for financial stability and freedom isn't straightforward. In Quadrant 1, your credit prowess is remarkable. Your house could be nearly mortgage-free or strategically rented to bolster your income. You're a cash car enthusiast, and college was funded with scholarships, sparing you student loan woes.

However, beware of the comfort trap. A cozy life, recurring expenses, and a comfort zone can lock you in. Escaping this zone can feel close to impossible. Partners might resist change, complicating the situation. At this stage, keeping your credit healthy and your income robust is paramount. Numerous strategies exist to achieve this, including growing passive income. But beware of moves that could accidentally shuffle you from Quadrant 1 to Quadrant 2.

Quadrant 2: High Income, Low Credit

Here's a quadrant that can be – anchored by a strong income yet entangled by maxed-out credit. The alluring whispers of Quadrant 1 might have pulled you in. For many contractors and blue-collar professionals, this becomes home as they advance in their fields. Incomes increase, families grow, and expenses follow suit. But what happens when the unexpected hits? Accidents and health issues – they can cut off your earning power. In Quadrant 2, the trap is real.

Quadrant 3: Low Income, High Credit

Now, the plot twist – Scenario 3 often offers a smoother path to financial freedom compared to Scenario 2. Incomes in this quadrant typically hover between 30k and 80k. Here, cautious living is the norm. Expenses are taken on thoughtfully without overburdening yourself. The belief that your earning potential is limited influences your choices. It's about finding comfort in your lifestyle, even if opulence isn't part of the equation.

Quadrant 4: Low Income, Low Credit

This scenario can either be the second toughest or surprisingly straightforward for achieving financial freedom. Bad decisions or a lack of support often land people here. Beware of the entitlement attitude that insists on being catered to. Sidestep these energy-draining people and focus on the resourceful ones. Some are used to adapting, fine with discomfort, and ready to seize opportunities. They're usually young and hungry for growth.

In essence, Quadrant 1 is akin to the "American Dream" – a life of luxury, vacations, and more. Quadrant 2 can deceive with the illusion of success. Quadrant 3, with good credit but limited income, offers surprising advantages. Quadrant 4 with bad credit and income can either trap you or offer an opportunity for growth. Keep company wisely and support the determined ones.

CHALLENGE |
THE FOUR FINANCIAL SCENARIOS

1. **Understanding Your Quadrant:** Take a moment to reflect on the descriptions of the four financial quadrants. Which quadrant do you think aligns most closely with your current financial situation? Remember, it's important to be honest with yourself – the goal is to accurately assess where you are right now.

2. **Identifying Your Strengths:** Consider the strengths and advantages of the quadrant you identified. What aspects of your financial situation are working well for you? Are there specific skills, habits, or decisions that have contributed to your current quadrant placement?

3. **Recognizing Potential Pitfalls:** Now, think about the potential challenges and pitfalls associated with your quadrant. What are the risks or vulnerabilities that come with your current financial scenario? How might these challenges impact your long-term financial goals?

4. **Setting Future Goals:** Given what you've learned about your current quadrant, take a moment to set some future financial goals. Where would you ideally like to be in the next 5 or 10 years? Is there a specific quadrant you aspire to move towards? What steps can you take to get there?

5. **Analyzing Your Strategy:** Based on the exercise, analyze your financial strategy. Are you on track to achieve your goals? Are there adjustments you need to make in your spending, saving, or investing habits to align with your desired quadrant?

6. **Exploring Your Network:** Look around your social circle and consider where your friends, family, or colleagues might fall in these quadrants. Does this exercise provide insights into their financial situations? How might understanding their quadrants help you offer better support or advice?

7. **Brainstorming Changes:** Finally, brainstorm a few changes or adjustments you can make to move closer to your desired quadrant. These could be related to improving your credit, increasing your income, managing expenses, or pursuing new opportunities. Create a short action plan for the next few months.

Remember, this exercise is a tool for self-reflection and strategic planning. It's okay if your current quadrant isn't where you want to be – the goal is to recognize your starting point and take steps to shape your financial future in a way that aligns with your goals and aspirations.

CHAPTER 5

DEFINING FINANCIAL FREEDOM

"If you want to be financially free, you need to become a different person than you are today and let go of whatever has held you back in the past."
— **Robert Kiyosaki**

When I was working at my first pest control job, going door-to-door, I was super excited and totally into it. If someone from a different company tried to contact me, I shut them down faster than they could send a message. My co-workers and I even joked about it, calling it "drinking the blue Kool-Aid."

Around the same time, I was reading "Think and Grow Rich," and I decided to make a 5-year plan for where I wanted to be and how much money I needed. I created a plan to make $500,000 in a year and have a bunch of passive income. But when I looked at what I needed to do to make it happen, I realized my current job wasn't the right fit. When I showed my boss, he just told me to lower my goals. That's when I knew I needed something more than the blue Kool-Aid.

The other day, I was going through my phone notes and saw that original goal. It was almost exactly five years ago, and guess what? I not only reached my goals but went beyond them. If you don't have clear goals, you won't get far.

Before we jump into how to switch from your current situation and make a plan to reach that "American Dream" of flexible work, let's figure out what financial freedom really means.

Stewart has always worked hard—mowing lawns and working while his friends hung out. He had just started college when he heard about other people getting internships. So, he quickly set up a Linke-dIn account to start looking, too. A few weeks later, he got a message from Michael Lanctot about a sales internship in another state, listed on LinkedIn—a platform he had just joined for class.

They set up an interview where Michael started asking Stewart about his goals and what he wanted to achieve.

"What would you do with $40,000?" Michael asked. "Uh, maybe save it. I hadn't really thought about it," Stewart said. "Cool, what are you saving up for?" Michael continued. "Investing, I guess," Stewart replied. "Nice, what kind of investments?" Michael inquired. "Houses and stocks. I want to make money without working," Stewart explained.

Michael persisted, "And why's that?" "So, I can be free from money worries," Stewart answered. "Awesome! How much money do you need to be free from money worries?" Michael asked. Stewart was getting a bit confused. Who was this guy asking all these questions? He thought he was being interviewed for a sales job. "Um, maybe like $20,000 to $30,000 a month," he guessed.

"Really? You'd need to make over $300,000 a year to have that. So, if you're making $10,000 a month without working right now, you're not truly free," Michael challenged. "Well, no, I still would be," Stewart argued. "Okay, then why $20,000 to $30,000 a month? What would you do with that money?" Michael probed. "Honestly, I'm not sure," Stewart admitted.

Michael said, "If you don't know where you're going financially, tough times might make you give up." Stewart was a bit confused because he thought this was a sales interview, not a life quiz. But then he realized he hadn't really thought much about his financial goals. Without a clear goal, you will keep wanting stuff but never really get anywhere. You need a clear goal to aim for, or else you'll keep going in circles.

Financial freedom and retirement can mean a lot of things. So, what's retirement? Does it mean chilling forever and then calling it quits? Retirement is simple—it's when you can stop working and still have enough money to live well. Your passive income is more than what you spend. For most people, it means their retirement savings can pay their bills until they're old. If you live longer, you might end up working at Walmart to not be a burden on your family.

Grant Cardone's early life was comfortable. His dad made good money, but when he suddenly passed away, things changed fast, and they went into Stage Four of the financial trap. Cardone's childhood became tough; he lost friends and struggled with addiction. If you looked at his life when he was 9 and then at 19, you'd wonder what happened. Maybe he would've still faced problems, but perhaps his wife wouldn't have had to work so much and clip coupons if they had more passive income. That's when I thought, "I need passive income, and I need it now." I spent months figuring out how to make sure my wife would be okay if something happened to me.

The first thing I did was figure out how much money we needed each month. Once I added up all the basics (rent, bills, insurance, and stuff), the plans started to take shape. My 2-year and 5-year plans began to come together. The crazy thing was, once I had those plans down, they didn't take as long as I thought they would. My 2-year plan ended up happening in just six months. Suddenly, I knew where I wanted to go and what steps to take to get there.

When you're making your financial plans, think of it like drawing a map. What stops do you need to hit? How do you get to those stops? It's important to have different 2-year and 5-year plans. For me, in 2 years, I want to make $50,000 a year without working all the time. To make that happen, I need to put in $250,000 and get a 20% return. I'm splitting that between Airbnb's, Turo's cars, and dividend stocks. In the first year, I need to get an extra $100,000 to put in. I'll do this by doing XYZ. Then, the investment will make me $20,000 passively. In the second year, I need to make $130,000 from my side hustles plus the $20,000 from last year. It's also good to know where this money is coming from.

Things might not go perfectly, so you might need to make more from your investments, spend less, or turn things you owe money on into things that make you money. My other 2-year plan is to make $50,000 a year without working all the time. I'll manage my Turo cars myself and take care of the Airbnb's, too, so they should make me 40%. On top of that, I'll rent out my car and spare room. So, my spare room is making $800 every month, and my car is making $400. That means I need to make an extra $37,600 every year. With a 40% return, I'll need to put in and make $94,000 over two years. I only need to make an extra $30,000 in the first year. With the $14,400 and the $12,000 from the previous year, I'd only need to make an extra $38,000 in the second year. And that's not even counting the passive income from year two.

Having many plans and being ready for whatever life throws at you is important. So, what gets you going? What motivates you? For me, back in college, I used to donate plasma between classes and during my morning job. I hated it. Every time I saw the scars from the needles on my arms, I knew I never wanted to go through that again. What about you? What motivates you? Take a moment to think about it. What did you believe financial freedom meant before today? Has your perception changed? Look around you – are the people you spend time with also striving for financial freedom? If not, maybe it's time to find a new crew.

Making Your 5 & 10-Year Plans

I'd like to share something I read that resonated with me when creating your 5- and 10-year plans. In the book "The 48 Laws of Power," the 18th law talks about not building a fortress to protect yourself. One of the examples is about a painter named Jacopo da Pontormo, a prominent artist during the Italian Renaissance.

In the mid-1500s, Pontormo was granted a massive commission by Duke Cosimo I de' Medici to paint the main chapel of Florence's Church of San Lorenzo. Eager to protect his work, he walled off the entire chapel to isolate himself. He spent eleven years painting alone, immersing himself entirely in the tiniest details of his painting.

But Pontormo died before he finished his work. When others finally saw what he had painted, they found a disoriented, chaotic piece. He lost sight of the larger picture in his intense focus on the individual strokes and shades.

I want to draw a parallel between this story and the journey of Elon Musk. We all know Musk as a mastermind of futuristic ideas and the founder of companies like Tesla and SpaceX. He's always thinking big, yet he's never lost in the details. His 5- and 10-year plans aren't just plans; they are grand visions—colonizing Mars, revolutionizing transportation, and pushing the boundaries of artificial intelligence. He comes up with the vision and creates a mastermind group of people who can turn that vision into reality. Nothing would get done if Musk got too caught up in the details.

Despite the enormous pressure and high stakes, Musk has never isolated himself. He is known to work alongside his teams, sleeping in factories and absorbing the details while keeping his eyes firmly on the larger picture. He's involved in each of his projects but is not sidetracked by them.

That's the kind of approach we need to adopt. In our day-to-day tasks, it can be tempting to isolate ourselves, particularly when we feel pressured or threatened. We might think that by shutting out the world, we can focus better and dive deeper into the details, but this approach is flawed. As Law 18 states:

"Never isolate yourself when you come under pressure. This cuts you off from the information you need and from people who could help you, and when real danger arises, you won't see it coming. Instead, make a point of being outgoing. Contact with others increases your power. Isolation is dangerous."

When we isolate ourselves, we close ourselves off from valuable resources, feedback, and perspectives and risk being blindsided by unforeseen challenges. We need to maintain our connections, reach out to others, and increase our power by connecting with other ambitious, like-minded people.

Dreams cannot come true without paying attention to details, but not at the expense of our larger mission and sense of purpose. We need to develop the discipline to always keep our eyes on the big picture—our 5- and 10-year plans.

So, take this lesson from "The 48 Laws of Power" seriously. Don't isolate yourself. Don't get lost in the details. Stay connected and engaged with your network, and maintain a balance between your daily tasks and your long-term objectives. By doing this, I'm confident we will not only reach but surpass your 5- and 10-year plans.

To drive this point home, I'd like to share a personal example. While I was listening to Napoleon Hill's book, "Think and Grow Rich," I started thinking about the life I wanted to create and began building a plan. At that time, I was working for a company and, like many, was intoxicated by the "Kool-Aid hype" about how great the company was. "Oh, they're the best of the best." I was very invested in their culture, but I saw a lot of guys making way less money than they could be. When I drafted my 5- or 10-year plan, I realized it wasn't achievable with that company. So, I moved to a place where it was possible.

After joining the next company, I expanded my 10-year plans because I knew I wanted to accomplish bigger things. However, when I expressed my intentions to scale with much bigger goals, the response I received was discouraging. "Oh, well, we don't think that's achievable, so you should probably just lower your goals or focus on some other things."

That was the biggest sign that it was time to go. Because if you can't figure out how you will achieve your 5- and 10-year goals doing what you're currently doing, then it will be incredibly demotivating. That's why building your 5- and 10-year plans is extremely important. It helps you measure and evaluate whether or not you're on track toward doing what you want to do.

Spend time thinking about the things you want to accomplish, especially those big-picture items that you want to build. Maybe you want to go on a church mission or have income-based goals. Maybe you want to buy properties or do other specific things. Also, consider what your 5-year plan would look like if you didn't hit your goal in year one or two. Better yet, imagine if you hit or even exceeded your goal: How would your 5- or 10-year plan change?

Based on these scenarios, I encourage you to have multiple plans. This will help you stay motivated and also prevent you from getting lost in the details. Having projections and a clear idea of your various pathways will allow you to adapt and pivot as necessary, keeping your eyes on the ultimate prize—your big-picture goals.

Let's all remember this lesson from Jacopo da Pontormo's story. Let's not get consumed by the details. Let's stay engaged, connected, and focused on our larger mission. Because we're not just creating individual brushstrokes; we're painting a masterpiece, and every stroke contributes to our grand vision for the next 5 and 10 years.

CREATING YOUR 5- & 10 YEAR PLANS

Step 1: Start with the End in Mind

5-Year Goal: Clearly define what you want to achieve five years from now. It could be anything—financial independence, running a successful business, publishing a book, or even personal milestones like building your dream home.

10-Year Goal: Go bigger. Where do you see yourself in a decade? It might be to scale your business internationally, retire early, or make a significant impact in your community.

Step 2: What Kind of Things Would You Like to Accomplish Along the Way?

Milestones for 5-Year Plan:

1. Year 1:

2. Year 2:

3. Year 3:

4. Year 4:

5. Year 5:

Milestones for 10-Year Plan:

1. Year 6:

2. Year 7:

3. Year 8:

4. Year 9:

5. Year 10:

Step 3: Where Are You at Right Now?

1. **Financial Status**: Assess your current financial health. If your goal involves a lot of capital, make plans on how to accumulate it.

2. **Skill Set**: What skills do you possess that will help you in this journey? Identify the skills you need to acquire or develop.

3. **Network**: Who in your current network can help you accomplish these goals? Aim to meet new people who can get you closer to your 5- and 10-year objectives.

4. **Resources**: Look at the tangible and intangible resources you have—time, money, influence, and so on. How can they be leveraged?

5. **Challenges**: Acknowledge the potential challenges you'll face and brainstorm solutions or workarounds.

Action Steps

- **Break Down Goals**: Split your milestones into smaller achievable tasks.

- **Timeline**: Create a realistic but flexible timeline for each task and milestone.

- **Accountability**: Find someone to hold you accountable. It could be a mentor, business partner, or even a dedicated client.

- **Review and Adapt**: Periodically review your plans. Life is unpredictable; be prepared to adapt your plans as you go along.

There you go! This is a fairly comprehensive strategy to set you on a path towards your 5- and 10-year goals. It's ambitious, but with the right mindset, you will get there.

CHALLENGE |
DEFINING FINANCIAL FREEDOM

1. Get Clear on Your Financial Goals: Don't just think about wanting "more money." Define what financial freedom looks like for you in numbers. How much do you need to make passively to cover your lifestyle? Write it down. Yes, actually write it down.

2. Create Your 2-Year and 5-Year Plans: Just like the article points out, break down your big vision into actionable steps. What investments or side hustles will get you to your financial freedom number? Work backwards to find out what you need to start doing today.

3. Evaluate Your Current Situation: Take an honest look at where you are right now. Is your current job or business going to help you reach your financial goals in the timeframe you've set? If not, consider what changes need to be made.

4. Build Your Financial Team: You can't do this alone, and as the article points out, isolation is dangerous. Who are the mentors, advisors, or friends that can guide you? If you don't have those people in your life right now, make it a point to find them.

5. Never Stop Revising: Once every quarter, revisit your plans. Celebrate the milestones you've hit, and make adjustments for the goals you haven't. Remember, the journey to financial freedom is not a straight line. Be prepared to adapt.

CHAPTER 6

MOVING THROUGH THE QUADRANTS

"All revenue is not the same. If you remove your worst, unprofitable clients and the now-unnecessary costs associated with them, you will see a jump in profitability and a reduction in stress, often within a few weeks. Equally important, you will have more time to pursue and clone your best clients."
~**Mike Michalowicz**

For three years after acquiring my home, I rented out two rooms on Airbnb in my first house. My mortgage was $1,100 a month, and my Airbnb rooms brought in $2,000 a month. I was making money just by living in the house! My wife wasn't a fan; we didn't have our private space or our cars because we rented them on Turo. However, our expenses were minimal, and we had a decent passive income. Our monthly costs were under $1,000. It's astonishing what can be achieved when your expenses are so low. By allowing ourselves this discomfort, we were able to move from Quadrant 4 to Quadrant 2 within a year.

Quadrant 1: High Income, High Credit

Quadrant 2: High Income, Low Credit

Quadrant 3: Low Income, High Credit

Quadrant 4: Low Income, Low Credit

"Dude, how did you get a house already? I've been making over 100k for the last few summers but still haven't been able to get one." Those were the words of a salesman I met from a different company while I was out knocking on doors. My mind was blown when he told me how much he was making and how he still didn't have a property of his own. After talking to him for a while, we realized he had an accountant who was very dedicated to finding every possible tax deduction for him.

Since he worked in door-to-door sales and was always traveling around, he had a ton of deductions. He had his LLC get paid rather than himself, and he took a general business tax deduction. He drove his car everywhere for work, so he racked up the miles, got deductions for living out of state, for his cell phone, for the bedroom in his rental he used as an office, and a million other things his accountant could think of to lower his taxable income.

After making over $100,000, his taxable income to the IRS was less than $30,000. I explained to him what DTI was and that when you're getting a property, the bank doesn't want your home loan to push you over 50%. Not only that, but he also had a $700/month car loan, and he only had one credit card he got just a year ago. I'm happy to report that he now has property and is acquiring more rental units as we speak. Many people in Quadrant 2 are also contractors—people who take all the deductions they possibly can to avoid paying taxes without realizing they're really shooting themselves in the foot.

I earned a significant income working for Edge Pest Control and heavily invested in my businesses. I saw the benefits of good credit, so I started W2ing my wife from one of our businesses. We were able to use her credit to acquire more rental properties and Turo cars. In two years, I moved from Quadrant 4 to Quadrant 1. However, this transition won't be as rapid for everyone. Over those two summers, I made hundreds of thousands of dollars from sales and management, and I had the entire "off-season" to manage my assets to increase their profitability. The point is that it's achievable. I managed to do it in two years. If I can do that, I can teach you how to do it in four, six, or ten years. However long it takes, it can happen.

My parents instilled an entrepreneurial spirit in me from a young age. They always involved us in Amway functions and encouraged us to read books like "Rich Dad, Poor Dad" and "How to Win Friends and Influence People." My mom runs a business where she sources local produce from farms in Colorado, Utah, and Texas and delivers it to areas with limited options. During the COVID pandemic, business exploded as people's needs increased and conventional methods fell short. She decided to expand her business by adding more trucks, extending her coverage, and renting a refrigerated storage space. However, as the pandemic subsided, so did her expansion.

Now, she had payments for trucks that were frequently in the shop and rent for a facility that she didn't need.

Like most people, she thought she needed to boost revenue and invest in advertising. After all, you can't make money without spending money, right? That's debatable, but we'll leave that for another time. My mom read a book called "Profit First," which helped her determine if her business was profitable and if changes were necessary. She realized that the cost of ads and distribution to a larger customer base ate up any new profit. She was busier but earning the same amount. The increased revenue didn't benefit her since her end goal wasn't to sell the business.

What she did next is what most people in Quadrants 2 and 4 struggle with: cutting costs. She reduced her business's routes and the volume of products. She built a refrigerated room in their house to run her business, saving thousands of dollars a month by eliminating rent. She also started subleasing one of the extra trucks since she couldn't sell it due to the downturn in the market. Things started to look up until my dad developed a heart murmur and couldn't manage the physical labor aspects of the business. To make matters worse, a shortage of car parts affected my dad's work, so they couldn't supply the cars they sold to the police, and his commission checks were on hold.

Without his help, there was no way she could manage all the routes. Now, the challenge was not about her business creating more income but about it not causing them to lose money. Most businesses go through these periods, and if you rely solely on your business for your financial well-being, it will fail. It might not be today or tomorrow, but it will happen eventually.

My parents managed to weather this challenging period because they recognized that they could utilize things they already had to increase their income while simultaneously cutting expenses. They eliminated their car and truck payments by renting them out, saving expenses and generating a profit. A few months later, my mom told me that their Turo cars had brought in $4,000 that month and were a significant help as they got their business back on track.

Transition from Quadrant 2 to Quadrant 1

You need to cut costs and utilize all that you have! Rent out your jet skis, four-wheelers, cars, and extra rooms. Get involved in an MLM to learn more about entrepreneurship and connect with others who desire growth. Use this extra income to fund new assets or pay off debts, thus improving your credit ability.

Moving from Quadrant 3 to 1

Lexi struggled as a single mother; she has three girls and, between working and school, didn't see the kids much. Her friend started renting out her cars on Turo and asked Lexi to take care of them because her house was in a better position. After managing the cars for a few months, she was able to save up enough for a car of her own. She saved everything she made from the new car and then purchased a second, third, fourth, etc. She has now quit her job, manages her Turo cars, and is able to be at home with the girls all day.

Lexi is a great example of Quadrant 3; she didn't have any debt, no house payments, no car payments, etc., so she had good credit usage capability, but she didn't have any extra income. She picked up a side hustle and used the money from that to go out and start getting passive income for herself. There were a million other things she could have used that money for, things that seemed like immediate issues that needed her attention. Her daughters needed new ballet shoes; summer camps were approaching, and she needed to save up for those; her own personal car might have a random malfunction, and her savings could be low.

For those trying to escape Quadrants 3 and 4, making more money is imperative and then using that money strictly for passive income. Focusing on cutting expenses for these people doesn't usually bear much fruit since their waste is relatively low. There are some things that they can do to cut expenses and build passive income at the same time. Looking at an expense report for someone in Quadrant 3, it will become apparent by the end of this book in what ways they can cut expenses.

- Rent: $1900 / month

- Health Insurance: $300 / month

- Food: $1800 / month

- Misc. items: $300 / month

- Car insurance: $140 / month

- Car maintenance: $50 / month

- Gas: $120 / month

- Utilities: $450 / month

- Phone: $40 / month

That's $5,100 a month before taxes or other basic expenses. It's easy to see why Millennials and Gen Z complain about Boomers telling us to work harder when the basics for a family run you over $60,000 a year. If this is your family, then you'd need to be making over $80,000 in passive income before you could be confident in your financial security. But there are ways to tip the scales, as we've touched on before. Start with what you have: rent out one of the rooms in your house and get a special keypad. Now, your biggest expense is making you money. Depending on your location, it could bring in anywhere from $300 to $1,400 a month. On average, my Airbnb rooms bring in $1,000 a month.

Become a licensed insurance agent and set yourself up with your plans. It takes 15 hours to study for the exam, and it's not very hard to pass. Now, you can set yourself up on a lower plan and make residual income from your health and car insurance. You could also start setting up others that you know, saving them money while creating income for yourself. Renting out your car on Turo can be risky, and that would be my last suggestion. Things happen on Turo, and even though they have insurance, if your car gets stolen or is in an accident, it could jeopardize your job. It's not something that you can afford to do at this moment. However, taking the risk or getting another car can be a great avenue since it "eliminates" your insurance cost and car payment while also bringing in an income.

Consider joining an MLM. They offer discounts on a lot of the products you'd be using anyway and provide a small kickback. Find one with products you like and would use, so you're not suffering while saving money. With a few simple changes like this, instead of needing to make an 80k passive income, you could bump it down to a 50k-60k income, depending on what you were able to do. Taking the money you're saving and investing it into another Airbnb or more Turo cars can help you get there quickly.

When going the Airbnb route, it's important to understand that most lenders don't accept your Airbnb income toward your DTI ratio. However, there are ways around it to keep your credit usage capability high. Create an LLC and have your Airbnb account pay that LLC. Then, create a lease for the rental property between your LLC and yourself. Make sure your LLC pays you the same amount every month into your account, and after a few months, you'll be able to start counting this money toward your DTI. Setting up an LLC in a state like New Mexico, Delaware, or Wyoming can be extra advantageous in this situation since it's harder for banks, or anyone, to see who owns the LLC. In these states, owners aren't required to provide member information. Keeping a healthy DTI is extremely important on your journey from Quadrant 3 to Quadrant 1.

After filing for bankruptcy at 23, I lost my credit, couldn't rent an apartment, and had a summer job starting in one month, so returning to a job back home was out of the question. I felt stuck, as if I couldn't do anything. My sister let us move into a spare room in her house for a month, and my mom had some work for me, driving her truck in her business. I was being sued in bankruptcy court, so any money I made went straight to a lawyer. I still had student loan payments from the degree I had finished the year before, and I had a wife of one year. I was deeply entrenched in Quadrant 4: low income, awful credit. It took me two years from that point to become a millionaire. I'm not saying this to brag but to offer hope to everyone in this quadrant who feels there's no way out. If you're in this quadrant, you'll need to utilize everything we've already discussed and likely more.

Here is a guide on steps to take.

Budget

The most important thing to do is to go through a budget for the necessities and determine how much you need to earn to survive. This will be your starting point for financial freedom. From there, you can expand it to include wants. Some of you will have liabilities that aren't easily eliminated, so these will need to be included in your necessary costs.

Find ways to utilize what you have. Consider renting out anything that wouldn't cost you, such as a room on Airbnb, a trailer, or a car. Understand that there are always associated risks, so have some safeguards in place. Your rental car could get totaled, you could have a squatter in your house, or someone could steal your trailer. Proper precautions will limit your exposure to these risks. Always have a separate checking or savings account for this money so you don't spend it impulsively.

Cut Costs

To become financially free, focus on eliminating all non-essential expenses, such as dining out, vacations, costly dates, and subscriptions. Also, consider ways to reduce ongoing costs, like finding cheaper insurance rates or using an older phone. You can even think about renting out assets you already have, like your car or spare rooms, to generate extra income. Place the money saved from these cuts into a separate account. This strategy isn't meant to last forever; it's designed to get you to a point where your passive income exceeds your expenses. Once you reach that milestone, you can start reintroducing some of the luxuries back into your life. There are many books that can guide you through this process.

Increase Income

There are many ways to increase your income. I love sales because you can determine your income. For some people, this is the easiest thing to do; for others, it's not. Increasing income generally means trading more time for money. If you have plenty of time, that's great. However, increasing income can be more challenging than cutting costs for those with families or significant others they want to spend time with. It requires juggling priorities. Make sure to maintain your relationships as you work to increase your income and get your significant other on board. Otherwise, you're in for a tough ride.

In the primary industry where I work, which is pest control, people often make big promises. One person will say, "Come with me, and you'll make $100,000," while another will claim, "Join me, and you'll earn $150,000." They talk about how to trade time for the most money. I chose a different path: I traded my money for unlimited time. This allowed me to create systems and processes that generate unlimited wealth.

Cut Taxes

Explore ways to reduce your tax liability with tax deductions and tax credits. This can be a game-changer. One of the biggest expenses people overlook is taxes, often seeing it as just an unavoidable cost of living. But have you ever wondered how the rich manage to sidestep those hefty tax bills? They've mastered the art of leveraging the tax code to their advantage.

Politicians create these tax codes with loopholes, often knowing that the average Joe won't figure them out. This way, they can give a leg up to their wealthy buddies while leaving the rest of us to foot the bill. If you don't want to be left behind, start educating yourself. Books like "Tax-Free Wealth" can be a good starting point. If you're earning through 1099, you've already got an edge; it allows you to find deductions that can lower your taxable income significantly.

But hey, it's not just about deductions; there are also tax credits, which are even better. Tax credits let you report a high income while still reducing your tax liability. The options are plenty, from solar tax credits to oil and gas incentives to credits for kids and education. And if you're planning to take out loans, make sure your Debt-to-Income ratio isn't negatively affected by all these deductions and credits. Staying on top of your tax game is crucial as you build your passive income streams. Deductions can cover a range of things, from a home office to travel expenses and mileage. So, as your income grows, make sure you're also doing everything you can to keep those taxes in check.

Improve Your Credit

Let's cut to the chase—your credit score is way more than just a number. It's like your financial passport, giving you access to opportunities or slamming doors in your face. Want to get a loan for that dream house or launch your startup with a business loan? Your credit score will either be your VIP pass or your biggest roadblock.

So, how do we turn this essential three-digit number into your personal golden ticket? By taking massive, intentional action, that's how.

Credit Building Strategies

Having good credit is a big piece in the puzzle of moving through the four quadrants. If you are just getting started with building credit or have had some setbacks with your credit and are feeling overwhelmed by your situation, relax; we've all been there.

Laying the groundwork: Doing online homework is the first step to turning things around. Search for "credit building strategies" and dig in. There are lots of great tips and tricks to get you off on the right foot. At the same time, getting your current financial house in order is crucial. Use Experian to check if you're behind on any bills. In fact, downloading Experian should be your first move in the quest to build solid credit. Let's break down a few proven methods to kickstart your credit-building journey. These are just brief explanations of what's possible. Do your own online research to see what makes the most sense for your situation.

Secured Credit Cards: First up, check out secured credit cards from big names like VISA, MasterCard, Discover, and American Express. These cards require a cash deposit, which typically sets your credit limit. They're a safe bet for lenders and a great starting point if your credit score is less than stellar. The best part? They report your payment history to the big three credit bureaus.

Store-Branded Cards: Next, consider snagging a store-branded credit card. Stores like Walmart and Target, or even gas cards, tend to be more lenient with approvals.

Leverage Trusted Relationships: Got a friend or relative with impressive credit? Ask to be added as an authorized user on their credit card. Their account will then show up on your credit file and report the entire history of that credit card from the date it was opened. Make sure it's a credit card at least five years old, and confirm they have no late payments on the account history. Your credit report will get a nice boost from their good habits, but be cautious— any negative marks on their account could affect you, too. Make sure you're an authorized user, not a co-applicant. This "credit piggybacking" lets you benefit from their positive payment history without actually using their card. Don't do this blindly. Do some research before you make this decision.

Diversify Your Credit Lines: Go for two secured cards to start. It diversifies your credit lines and amps up your score. Use them for necessities like gas and groceries, then pay them off immediately. Aim to have about five cards eventually, but take it slow; each new account can cause a temporary score dip.

Credit Utilization: Keep an eye on your spending. Try not to exceed 50% of your credit limit on any card. So, if you have a $500 limit, keep your spending below $250.

The Smart Way to Carry a Balance: Here's a little trick: When you pay off your monthly balance, leave a dollar or two unpaid. It might seem odd, but this small balance can boost your credit score by showing credit activity. But make sure you pay off this small balance after two business cycles because when you carry a balance, depending on your card type, it may result in interest charges on new transactions.

Use Experian Boost: You can quickly boost your credit report with Experian Boost. This game-changing, free service instantly elevates your credit scores by counting your everyday bills—like your cell phone, utilities, streaming subscriptions, and even your rent—toward your credit history. It's a hassle-free way to improve your creditworthiness.

After you check your Experian report, look at the marketplace and start getting any credit cards you can to begin building your credit history (try to get 5). Make sure to apply for all of them on the same day so that it has less of a negative effect on your credit report. The next step is making sure you're paying off those cards before they accrue any interest; leaving a dollar on the balance can help boost your credit faster. Make sure you're not closing out accounts too quickly; part of your report examines the length of time you have accounts open. Try to keep them all open for at least two years.

In a Nutshell: Credit is essentially a life hack; it lets you leverage other people's money to your advantage. Think of building credit as establishing your financial reputation. When you use credit wisely and strategically, it can catapult your financial progress into hyperdrive. The golden rule? Don't use credit as a replacement for income. Instead, make sure you use it as leverage to build your assets and passive income. Ultimately, your debt's ROI (return on investment) should outpace the interest you're shelling out on the loan.

How Good Credit Can Help: If I buy a car for Turo, like a Subaru Ascent, I buy the Subaru with a $1,000 down payment. The payment is either $650 or $700. Plus, there's $200 a month for insurance, so it's about $900 per month. On Turo, though, it's going to bring me $1,500. Within two months, I had a 100% return on my cash—the $1,000 I put in—and now it's generating income for me. Have you thought about that? It's $600 a month. That's $7,200 a year that it's generating for me.

So, you get a little tricky with it. You set up these businesses so that one business pays you a certain amount of "X-ray" income. You don't count the Turo income as your personal income; it goes to your business and pays you. After you own a few, you're pulling in $5,000, $6,000, or $7,000 a month, every single month.

Oh, and if you're smart, you set it up in one of the states like New Mexico, Delaware, or Wyoming, where you don't have to disclose owner information. This means banks won't be able to see that you own the company when you're applying for new loans. They won't be able to find that information, so they won't count your Turo income.

With $1,000 in credit, you can generate more than $7,000 in income. On top of that, you're building equity in that car. After six or seven years, the car will be worth about $25,000. So, think about it: a $1,000 investment creates $30,000 to $35,000, plus $25,000 if you sell it at the end of that period. That means $1,000 turns into $60,000 because of credit. That is why credit is amazing and why you need to utilize it.

Not only does credit help you build passive income in Turo, but it can also help you build passive income through getting rental properties, Jet Ski rentals, boat rentals, etc. However, this is extremely risky. There's no telling if you'll need to evict tenants or if someone will wreck your boat or car. You'll have to cover the car payments and insurance while the insurance sorts itself out. Make sure you understand the risks and have enough of a cash buildup before taking full advantage of credit.

Get Rid of Broken Financial Vehicles

Sometimes, life puts you in a position where you need to make difficult decisions, especially when it comes to your finances. Getting rid of broken financial vehicles, no matter the cost (even if it leads to being sued or filing for bankruptcy), can be a sound decision. It's crucial to own your circumstances rather than attributing your financial woes solely to "wasting money," especially if that's not actually the case.

The Case of Joe "J.D."

Take the example of Joe "J.D." who initially worked in sales for a company that continuously delayed his pay. Ultimately, the company went bankrupt, and so did J.D. He then started a labor-intensive but logically planned production company. However, he realized that wasn't his calling. J.D. then shifted gears entirely and went into the rewarding but demanding field of nursing. Now, he's toying with the idea of venturing back into entrepreneurship.

J.D. invested in a life insurance retirement plan (LIRP) because he's the conservative type. He also dabbles in sharing his car on Turo and has dipped his toes into real estate. Yet he finds himself unable to fully transition from an employee mindset to that of an entrepreneur.

So, what's J.D.'s next step?

In J.D.'s case, his broken financial vehicles were his initial sales job and perhaps his short-lived produce company. Holding onto these broken systems would have sunk him further into financial distress. It's like driving a car with a failing engine; no matter how much gas you pour into it, you're not going anywhere.

J.D. recognized the need to jump ship and did so by switching careers. He also cautiously ventured into other financial avenues, such as LIRP, Turo, and real estate. However, he's at a crossroads. He could stick with nursing, which is stable but possibly not his passion, or take another leap into entrepreneurship, armed with more experience and financial cushioning this time.

Evaluate and Eliminate: To proceed, J.D. — and anyone in a similar situation — should take a hard look at their financial vehicles. Are they propelling him towards his financial goals or holding him back? If he identifies broken vehicles, cutting them loose is crucial, even if it means facing legal consequences or bankruptcy.

Imagine you're holding onto stock in a company that's consistently losing value. You might hold on, hoping things will improve, but sometimes it's smarter to sell at a loss and move your money into more promising ventures. Similarly, if J.D. finds that his dabbles in

Turo or real estate are draining his resources without adequate return, he should consider pulling out.

Lessons from Bankruptcy: It's easy to see bankruptcy as a failure, but sometimes it's a necessary reset button. It allows you to get rid of your debts and broken financial vehicles and gives you a fresh start. Returning to old, destructive habits is not a free pass. Bankruptcy is a chance to own your financial past and plan a better future, as J.D. did by re-evaluating his career path and financial investments.

The path to freedom is fraught with decisions that may seem counterintuitive, such as severing ties with a failing investment or even declaring bankruptcy. However, the decision becomes clearer when weighed against the lifetime financial burden that a broken vehicle could impose. Take stock of your financial vehicles, and don't be afraid to take drastic measures if they're not taking you where you need to go. Own your circumstances, learn from them, and move forward more wisely.

CHALLENGE I
MOVING THROUGH THE QUADRANTS

Get ready to flex those financial muscles and make some impactful moves.

1. **Dial Down the Expenses:** First up, take a good look at your current quadrant. You've got this! Identify ways to trim and reduce those expenses by a specific amount. Crunch those numbers and figure out how much you can realistically save. Then, calculate the impact on your income-to-expense ratio. This is your chance to balance the equation and level up your financial game.

2. **Boost Your Income, Cut Those Costs:** Now, let's tackle challenge number two. Think creatively. How can you increase your income while simultaneously cutting those costs? Brainstorm those ideas, and don't hold back! Write down actionable steps you can take to bring in more money while keeping your expenses in check. It's a win-win situation waiting to happen.

3. **Supercharge Your Income:** Challenge number three, folks! Get ready to up your income game. Imagine the possibilities. How can you take your income to the next level? Crunch the numbers and see by what amount that will affect your income-to-equity ratio. This challenge is all about envisioning a brighter financial future and making it happen.

4. **Credit Power-Up:** Time for a credit check-in! Challenge four is all about that credit score. What immediate action steps can you take right now to boost your credit? Think about it and jot down

those strategies. Remember, a strong credit score opens doors to better opportunities.

5. **The Credit Boost Blueprint:** Challenge number five, here we go! List out five solid ways you can enhance your credit score, starting today. These could be small but impactful actions that contribute to a healthier credit profile. And don't just leave it at that – make a game plan for the next week on how you're going to put these credit-boosting strategies into action.

6. **Broken Financial Vehicles:** Take a close look at your life and your finances. What are your broken financial vehicles that you need to reevaluate? This is an important conversation you need to have with yourself.

7. **BONUS: Learn from the Pros:** This one's a bonus round for the go-getters! Challenge yourself to observe the people around you. Identify how they've successfully increased their income, slashed expenses, and improved their credit. Take note of their strategies and successes, whether it's your friends, family, or colleagues. This is a fantastic way to learn and adapt to your own financial journey.

CHAPTER 7

MAKING MONEY ON PAPER VS. REALITY

"To achieve what 1% of the world's population has (Financial Freedom), you must be willing to do what only 1% dare to do: hard work and perseverance of the highest order."
— **Manoj Arora**

As you begin your journey to financial freedom, it's important to ensure you're making a profit. It's very easy to make the mistake many people make: having businesses or side hustles that bring in cash flow but don't actually make a profit. You can't rely on an accountant to tell you if it's profitable either, since what's on paper doesn't necessarily reflect the reality of your profitability.

I was helping a client with their Turo business after they got their sixth car. They were confused because their accountant said their Turo business was negative, and when they looked through it, they thought they were losing money, too. I calculated that my personal cars had a return of 50-80%, so I figured their accountant did what accountants do and factored in a lot of things that wouldn't apply to the business when looking at ROI.

I asked a pretty simple question: "Does your account go up or down?" They didn't know! They had that income going into their main account, so it was very difficult to figure out. I instructed them to create an LLC for extra tax benefits and taught them how to register the cars with an LLC. Once they did that, they had the Turo money going into that new business account.

We met up again a month later to review their account. On the surface, the account value was going up, so it was puzzling why they felt they were in the "negative." After going through the details, we realized the accountant had accounted for several expenses, like the depreciation of cars, meals out, and even parking fees the business paid to the owner.

While this was excellent accounting for tax purposes—because it included all these possible deductions—it didn't accurately reflect their actual financial situation. For example, the cars weren't really losing value as quickly as the depreciation claimed. Also, using mileage for depreciation can result in bigger deductions if you have fewer than four cars. Plus, they weren't incurring extra parking costs at their own home, and the meals out would have been a regular expense anyway.

When we got down to it, we found out his business had a 40% ROI. Not only was he getting an increase in cash, but he also wasn't having to pay taxes on it because of all the deductions! There can be a reverse situation too. Your books can say you're making a profit, but when you look at your account, it's empty. *If you're in this scenario, you should first read the book, "Profit First."* Ways this can happen are very simple: you have a lot of unqualified expenses that don't count for deductions. Because of this, you're not deducting the income and still showing a profit. Make sure your businesses focus on any expenses that will bring deductions, and make sure to avoid any costs that don't bring deductions.

Having businesses that are "negative on paper" can be a huge plus. For example, when Elon Musk purchased SolarCity, many people thought he was an idiot because they thought he tanked the company. It reported massive losses, and during that time, they were also "renting" out panels, so the company was able to keep the solar tax credit for themselves. One of the biggest "losses," and the things people criticized Elon for, actually saved him billions of dollars in taxes. He received billions in subsidies and credits from the government during the purchase. Taxes will wreck you, but there are a lot of good ways to avoid them.

A lot of people like to flaunt their money and flaunt what they have, and it can be a good tactic for recruiting and building attraction. However, when it is taken too far, it will jeopardize your financial security. When you're looking at making money on paper versus actually making money (profit), you might be saying, "Okay, I can spend this money here, and I can flaunt my money there, and I can spend this much because it will make me more money," but it will get out of hand. Most of the time, it does not deliver.

For example, there's an attractive solar company that some of my salesmen have worked for. At the time, they were doing installations quickly. The incentives were insane. The owner of the business was new to owning a company, and he was super flashy. He put a Lamborghini on Instagram, and everyone thought he was making crazy money, and it was amazing. A lot of my salesmen didn't get paid on the deals that got installed. The money never hit their bank accounts, and the company ended up filing for bankruptcy.

On paper, the solar company was making a ton of money. Reputable people in the industry were getting into the business and then getting out right away. They saw on paper that this company was making money, but when they actually got into it, they could see that the company was bleeding money and that the owner of the company was making terrible decisions, destroying the company from within. Don't get caught up in the trap of feeling like you're making money on paper and feeling like you're progressing but not actually making money.

Now, in addition to making money in reality versus on paper, you also need to understand where your time is best spent. On paper, if you're going out and fixing something on your house or driving to save money instead of flying, is it saving you money? In reality, what is your time worth? If you were doing something else during that time instead of driving, if you were working or marketing your talents, would it be getting you more money?

For example, my brother's an electrical engineer who makes $100 an hour. He was going out and doing some work on one of his cars. And I said, "Jacob, what are you doing? Why are you working on your car?" And he said, "Well, you know, the mechanic wanted X amount of dollars." So, we broke it down: on paper, he was saving money, but in reality, it cost him money to do that.

What is your time worth? You need to understand what your talent and time are worth. And what you can do with your time: when you're marketing your skills, working at your job, or doing whatever you're doing, is it making you money on paper? Are you saving money on paper? Or are you saving and making money in reality? That is a very important distinction.

One of the most common things that my salesmen get into is that they'll go and shadow and spend time with the wrong sales reps. And I would explain to them, "Hey, if this salesman increases by this much, how much money will that make you? Why are you not knocking yourself? Why are you doing that? Are you really making the best use of your time? On the flip side, if you're knocking by yourself and not helping your salesmen at all, you're missing out on leveraging their efforts to boost your income. You're going to make more money from helping your sales than you will from your personal sales. You have to think about where your time is best spent. Where will you get the highest ROI on your time, and where will you actually be making the most money?"

Understanding these principles is crucial to achieving financial freedom. Once you grasp the difference between making money on paper and in reality and know where to best spend your time, you'll reach financial freedom faster. Understanding these principles and learning how to make the best use of your time is a must. Your road to financial freedom will be filled with a lot fewer bumps, a lot fewer detours, and a lot less time wasted.

CHALLENGE |
MAKING MONEY ON PAPER VS. REALITY

1. **Time vs. Money**: Take a moment to reflect on how you're investing your time. It's not just about obvious time-wasters like video games and TV. Think deeper. Identify activities that seem financially promising but might actually be draining your resources. Consider whether these activities align with your financial goals and whether they're truly worth the investment of your precious time.

2. **Unveiling the Illusions**: Think about people you've come across who appeared financially successful on the surface, but their ventures didn't match the hype. Dive beneath the glossy exterior and dissect the reasons behind their financial disconnect. What lessons can you glean from their experiences? This exercise will sharpen your ability to spot genuine opportunities and avoid shiny but empty promises.

3. **Mastering the Tax Game**: Explore the realm of tax optimization. Are there clever strategies you can employ to reduce your taxable income on paper while boosting your actual earnings? Delve into ways to maximize deductions and credits without jeopardizing your financial stability. Seek advice from mentors or advisors who've mastered these tactics, even if their visible income doesn't mirror their genuine wealth.

Engaging with these challenges will deepen your financial acumen and empower you to align your strategies with real-world outcomes. Remember, the journey to financial freedom is paved with well-informed decisions and a profound understanding of how your choices shape your tangible results. Keep pushing forward and watch your financial future flourish!

CHAPTER 8
BUSINESS AND LIVELIHOOD

"Until your money starts working for you,
you will always be working for your money."
— **Linsey Mills**

Let's dive into the tale of Luigi's Pizza Shop to unpack some hard truths about running a small business. When COVID-19 made its grand entrance, it wasn't just a health crisis; it turned into an existential crisis for many businesses. Panic swept through communities, causing a domino effect of closures. Many businesses folded, mainly because they had not planned for an emergency of this scale. Their business and personal finances were intertwined, and there wasn't a safety net in sight.

Take Mark, the owner of Luigi's Pizza Shop. He was navigating through a maze of rumors about government help, unsure if his small business would even qualify. As foot traffic dwindled and staff members stopped showing up, the governor's stay-at-home order felt like the final blow. The business that Mark had poured years into was suddenly on the brink of collapse. Three long months passed with almost no business, draining all of his savings. Mark faced the grim reality: he could no longer afford his mortgage, much less the restaurant's overheads.

A well-meaning friend took to social media, urging everyone to help keep Luigi's afloat by ordering pizzas. When I walked in to pick up my order, the stress etched on Mark's face told a story of its own. "It's been so hard," he said. "Thank you so much for your business; it means more than you know."

So, why do businesses like Luigi's struggle? Most of the time, it's not about the quality of the product or service. Often, it's because the owners are financially dependent on the business for their livelihoods. The harsh lesson here is clear: you need to separate your personal and business finances if you want any shot at long-term success.

The Quest for Passive Income

Now, let's pivot a bit. While Mark's story highlights the dangers of relying solely on active income from your business, it also nudges us to think about the alternative: passive income. You know that magical money that flows in without you having to clock in and out every day? But be warned, getting to this stage is often easier said than done.

The underlying principle of passive income is that you don't have to work for the money. This right here is the whole idea. However, before we go any further, you need to know that building passive income is often easier said than done. Now, you already have an idea of what passive income is, and I'm pretty sure that you're capable of identifying whether or not you created it for yourself. So, we're not going to waste time going into those details.

What we will spend some time on is determining what you need to do if you come to the conclusion that you don't have passive income. Well, there's no need to panic since you're a couple of steps ahead of Luigi. You're at least aware of your and your business's financial position. The first thing that you need to do is identify ways to create passive income. To do this, you need to look at what your family, friends, and business competitors are doing.

Do they have passive income? How many sources of income do they have? What are those sources? Could you implement similar things in your professional and personal lives? As you reflect on those around you, these are all the questions you need to answer. However, this is not where you stop. Once you've answered these questions, give yourself some time and ponder upon the sources of income you haven't considered yet and the sources others around you aren't using just yet.

This is the time to put your thinking hat on because coming up with such sources of potential income will require some creativity.

Doing what others do to build passive income might work pretty well for you in your personal life, but the effectiveness of this approach is somewhat limited when it comes to businesses. To create passive income through your business, you need to have something new for your customers. It can be a sales channel you haven't used yet or a completely new product altogether.

The underlying fundamental for success in business is differentiation. Think about it: If you're offering the same thing that's on sale at the shop around the corner, why would customers come to you? They won't, and that's why you need to have something different. This often involves coming up with "out of the box" business ideas and implementing innovative business strategies. You need to figure out what your customers need and what other businesses aren't offering. Once you have that down, you need to offer it in a way that no one else can. But this isn't passive income. It's just offering something new! It'll only be passive income when your business can sustainably generate that income without your involvement.

Now, move on to safeguarding your livelihood. You need to identify potential risks in both your personal and professional lives that can impact and deteriorate your financial position. Think about some events that could disrupt your income. Make a list, but don't just stop there. Figure out a couple of major events that are not likely to happen, but if they do, they can cause your income to decline severely or even be eliminated altogether. Lastly, focus on developing a plan for how you can mitigate or tackle these risks. Take some time out to create an emergency fund to safeguard your livelihood. Learn new skills and diversify your income so you can have steady cash flow during adversity.

Financial Resilience

By understanding the lessons from Luigi's Pizza Shop and recognizing the value of passive income, you can better position both yourself and your business for financial resilience and success. So, if you're reading this and realizing you're a couple of steps ahead of Mark—because you're at least aware of your financial situation—

then there's room for optimism. Start by looking around you. What are your family, friends, and competitors doing to create passive income? What kind of income streams have they set up? Take note and see if there are any that you could adopt or adapt for your own situation. The objective is to create sufficient passive income and a self-sufficient lifestyle that allows you to keep your business and personal livelihood entirely separate.

Consider Elon Musk and Tesla. The business that made Elon Musk the world's richest man almost failed multiple times. He invested everything he had into it without taking anything out. It was on the brink of failure when NASA contracted Tesla and saved the business. If he had withdrawn money from the business even once, there's a high chance it would have failed.

We've talked about your goals—why you want financial freedom. You don't have to do it through Airbnb, Turo cars, etc., but you do have to do it through passive income before you can really scale a business.

Here's the question you need to ask yourself: Now, at this moment, decide: Do you want that financial freedom, or do you want to actively work your business? And by that, I mean that for some of you, you may just want to run your business. You've developed enough skills where you feel like you're set. Don't do it. That is putting yourself back in the trap. Without financial security and financial freedom from passive income, every second you go out and work, you are in jeopardy of getting your neck snapped by the trap.

Don't fall for it. If you want a business, it doesn't matter if you don't want to scale. You don't have to think about it. "Oh, I want to scale huge." Your financial survival depends on you going out and creating passive income for yourself to support your livelihood. There's nothing wrong with going out and running a business doing something you love to do. It's great if your plumbing business can support you, but have you built your business correctly so it can create passive income? What happens if your leg breaks? What happens if you die? Will it continue to generate income for your husband or wife or for your family? These are the kinds of questions that you have to be thinking about. It's okay if you want to be a plumber or anything like that, but make sure you set it up so that it is passive. You may not be able to scale it, but that's okay.

A lot of people think they don't want to be Elon Musk. They don't want to be huge. They just want to have a small operation. It's okay for them just to do their thing, run their new clients, and not go huge, right? So why would they need the passive income? It's not about that. It's about financial security for your family and for yourself. If you've got a business that relies on you for operations, that's awesome; you're just self-employed, right? It's not creating passive income. If you're having to actively work in there, then you're not set, and your family is not secure.

The entire reason you have to get financially set and secure is so that no matter what happens, if there's a pandemic or some kind of new technology that makes your job or your self-employment obsolete, you're still financially set. That is why you need this. Luigi had no idea there could be a pandemic and a stay-at-home order, and that has tanked his situation, right?

You don't know what's going to come around the corner, so you need to diversify your passive income. You need to have multiple sources of income that can support you in the event of some kind of economic change, because it will always happen. Rather than fearing, "Oh, what if this happens, what if this happens," set yourself up to be like, "Okay, no matter what happens, I'm set." So that's a better way to live.

The All-In Approach to Building Passive Income

One of the most important things to remember when you're starting to build your passive income is that you have to be all-in. The more committed you are, the quicker you'll achieve your financial goals.

Many people treat generating passive income as a hobby. That's a mistake. You must invest not only your money but also your time and energy into building this income stream. It has to be your main focus.

I mentioned earlier in the book that in my first few years as a homeowner, my wife and I rented out extra rooms in our house through Airbnb. This is a perfect example of being all-in on building passive income. Yes, it was uncomfortable at times, but we knew we wanted to build passive income, and we had to start with what we had and build from there. Do we have to do that now? Of course not, but when we made that decision to rent out rooms in our home, sacrificing privacy, what we were really doing was committing to the all-in mindset.

When first starting out, sacrifices are necessary. Don't think for a second that you'll make a substantial impact quickly without making sacrifices. Forget about:

- Going on trips

- Having 'fun money'

- Engaging in extra leisure activities

However, if you can endure these sacrifices and invest wisely for a couple of years with an all-in mindset, you can achieve financial freedom for the rest of your life.

Bumps and Detours

Diving into passive income is often a journey filled with bumps and detours, but man, it's worth it. People often hesitate because they're afraid of making mistakes or failing. But like you said, "Every complex system starts simple." You don't have to start with a grandiose business model. You can kick things off small and then scale up as you learn the ropes.

Think about it: nobody becomes a real estate mogul overnight. You might start with a single rental property or even just rent out a room in your home on Airbnb. The point is to get started and learn along the way. Even if you don't get it right the first time, you'll gain valuable experience that will make the next try that much easier.

Let's not forget about investments like stocks, bonds, or cryptocurrency. Yeah, the market can be volatile, but the sooner you dip your toes in, the sooner you'll start understanding how it all works. Even if you only invest a small amount initially, you're setting yourself up for potential long-term gains.

The Imperfect Start

Aiming for perfection is often the enemy of progress. The ideal moment to start will never come if you're waiting for all the stars to align. Start with what you've got, where you're at. Maybe your first rental property isn't a luxurious villa, and that's okay. It's more about understanding your numbers—can you cover the costs and still make a bit on top? If yes, then it's a good place to begin. Financial freedom doesn't demand a perfect start; it requires a start, period.

Don't let the fear of imperfection hold you back. Anything worth doing is worth doing poorly at first. Mistakes are not only inevitable but also invaluable. You learn the most when things don't go as planned. So, take the leap, embrace the learning curve, and start building that passive income stream.

Finding Mentors

Mentorship is like a shortcut through the labyrinth of life's challenges. Whether it's a friend who's already playing the real estate game or an online guru in affiliate marketing, mentors can offer you lessons that they learned the hard way. Of course, quality advice often comes with a price tag, but it's an investment in your future. On the other hand, if you do stumble upon free advice from someone who genuinely cares about your growth, latch on! That's pure gold.

Invest in Yourself Through Education

Look, nobody's going to invest in you if you're not willing to invest in yourself. Taking specialized courses or attending industry seminars broadens your perspective and puts you in the same room as like-minded individuals. And yes, Benjamin Franklin nailed it: turning your money into wisdom will eventually turn back into even more money. Consider each class or seminar as another stepping stone toward your financial goals.

The People You Keep and the Hustle

Your social circle can be a launchpad or an anchor. Childhood friendships are great, but they don't always withstand shifts in ambition and lifestyle. As you climb the ladder, some will cheer you on, others will mysteriously disappear, and a few might even try to pull you down. The sooner you recognize who's who, the better you can focus on your path.

On Friendships and Grinding

The grind will act as a filter for your relationships. Listen to those who are where you want to be, not those who hold you back with their own limitations. When someone questions your decisions, especially if they're not financially where you aspire to be, take it with a grain of salt. It's your journey, and the people advising you should ideally be those who've traveled a similar path successfully.

Be Selective in Whose Advice You Take

Trust is earned, not given, and especially so when it comes to advice that could shape your future. The financial advice from your neighbor Bob, who has never invested in anything riskier than a savings account, probably isn't what you want to stake your future on. Keep your circle tight and your advisors tighter. Aim for advice from those living the life you want, not those who have settled for less.

Negativity Be Gone!

Life's too short to be surrounded by naysayers. If someone is consistently raining on your parade, it's time to pack up and find a new route. And you don't have to make a big fuss about it—simply distancing yourself might be enough. Your journey toward financial freedom is your own; don't let anyone dim your light because they're uncomfortable with how bright you're shining.

CHALLENGE |
BUSINESS AND LIVELIHOOD

1. Passive Income Inventory: Take a moment to list the different forms of passive income you currently have. Whether it's rental properties, investments, royalties, or any other source – jot them down.

2. Observing Others: Reflect on the people around you. What types of passive income do they have? Are there any sources you haven't considered yet?

3. Creativity Unleashed: Brainstorm creative ways to acquire passive income. Consider unconventional yet promising opportunities you've come across or innovative businesses that generate passive income. Think about the inventive strategies you've seen others implement.

4. Identifying Risks: Delve into potential factors that could jeopardize your financial security. What are some situations or events that could disrupt your income streams or financial stability? Think beyond the obvious to pinpoint hidden risks.

5. The White Swan Event: Imagine a "white swan" event – a rare but impactful incident that could catch you off guard. What could this event be, and how might it affect your financial well-being? Get specific about its potential consequences.

6. Preparing for the Unknown: Develop a plan to safeguard against these risks. How can you proactively mitigate the impact of these challenges? Consider strategies to diversify your income, build

an emergency fund, or acquire new skills to adapt to changing circumstances.

Engaging with these challenges will refine your understanding of passive income and bolster your ability to safeguard your financial future. Remember, the path to financial security involves both creativity and preparation. So, dive in, explore, and emerge with a more robust financial strategy!

CHAPTER 9
THE POWER OF FINANCIAL SECURITY

Financial security doesn't come from the amount of money you currently have; it comes from your ability to get more of it whenever you want. Master the art of serving others and you will secure your financial future.
—**Michael Neill**

When I think of Elon Musk, after he became financially secure, he never had to take money from Tesla and put it into his other businesses. Instead, he has used his own personal money to invest in his businesses. He's only been able to do that because he was financially secure.

So, when I talk to people about building financial security, many of them who are interested in that and with whom I work want to build businesses. They want to be able to grow their businesses without the fear of, "Hey, am I going to be able to feed myself? How am I going to be able to do this?"

The goal is that if I can get myself financially set—financially secure and free through multiple layers of passive income—then it doesn't matter if my business fails or has setbacks. For me, the ultimate financial freedom is having multiple streams of income that could each independently support my needs in life. Right? And then, obviously, I'd have a surplus when they're all doing well.

Here's why having passive income has been so important for me, and you can use my setup as an example for creating your own situation. I have a large summer team I run and must take care of. I won't get a single paycheck until next February because I'm no longer knocking on doors; I'm off the doors. So, I go a year without a single paycheck. I can manage my life and business this way because I have built up enough passive income from different forms of real estate, like Airbnb, rental properties, and Section 8. I also have income from leasing out cars and some other income sources.

At one point, I found myself in a tricky situation because I used bad judgment. I had allowed some people I know to rent out their own cars on my Turo business account. They didn't maintain their cars very well, and it tanked my reviews. Turo is set up so that if your 5-star ratings dip to 80% or less, they suspend your account. Because these other people were not staying on top of their car maintenance, they suspended my account, which hit me hard because that was a huge income source for me—a decent six-figure income from my Turo business—and it was just instantly gone.

Initially, it was like, "Oh my gosh, this sucks," but it wasn't that bad because I still had all my money coming in from my leased cars. I still had all my money coming in from my rental properties, from my Section 8, and from my Airbnb. And so, I was still able to support our needs.

The power of having these multiple streams of income, all of which could support my life, is a great example of what you can do for yourself. Yes, we had to cut back a little bit that month, but we were still going to be fine, and I'm still going to be able to focus on the things that are going to make me more money. Because, at the end of the day, I focus on my other businesses that are growing, like my greenhouse business and touring around the country to work with all my reps in the summer—because summertime business is essential, it's my big focus because it's my February payday. During the summer, my attention must be on my guys, not my other businesses. Because I have multiple income streams, I can focus on my guys.

That's how I went from making $200,000 in personal and overrides last summer to making a million dollars in overrides this summer. Because last summer, I had to knock; I couldn't focus on my guys and scaling my team. I ended up with passive income from one stream, but not enough to feel completely secure in stepping out to scale my summer pest control business. So I built up those other streams, and then I was able to go out and launch myself into that next level, going from $200,000 to a million.

Before that, I had another situation where having passive income helped me out. I was working for Edge Pest Control. They were making some decisions I didn't really like, which affected my production with them. My Turo and Airbnb businesses were going well, and I realized, "You know what? I don't like the decisions you guys are making. I'm going to take a step back. I'm just going to focus on my other businesses," and the freedom to do that was built in because of my passive income.

Yes, my income from Edge took a hit. I ended up not getting most of my door money. I ended up not getting my backend because there's a built-in fine if you were a manager and you didn't finish out with them. So, I didn't get that large part of my backend. But it was fine; it was like $70,000 that I missed out on, but it was okay because I did what was right for me, and I had my passive income coming in.

Now, fast forward: because I did that, I was able to work for Hawks the next year. And that allowed me to go out and make $500,000. At the last company, I would not have made nearly that much money. And then the next year, going out and not having to knock any more, I made $400,480. Let's just say $500,000. Being able to go out and not having to knock any more, I could just focus on growing and scaling my guys. My business was able to grow, and we made a million dollars. Before, I only did 3 million in revenue, and then I went up and did 10 million in revenue.

Those are the kinds of drastic changes and drastic expansions you can create when you have financial security. That is the real power: you can take risks and afford to lose. You can bet big, and you're fine if it doesn't work out. Risk-taking is how you succeed; it's how you make money.

Look at the wealthy: they take big risks, and they succeed because their financial freedom gives them the time to leverage their money.

On the flip side, the dangers of not having passive income and financial security are that you never know what life is bringing. I think of Grant Cardone; I've heard him talk about his difficult upbringing that was ravaged by drugs, drinking, and crime—a lot of things that often come from being raised in a single-parent household. That's not how his life started, though. His parents were very well off. They had a lake house, a boat, and tons of toys. His father passed away completely unexpectedly when he was young, and his mom was left with all these liabilities, no income, and no way to get income since she had to take care of the kids. She had been taking care of them for years as a stay-at-home mom, so she didn't have any easily monetizable skills.

You don't know what is going to happen in life; what you do know is that there's a possibility that something will happen to you. And if it happens, do you want to leave your family in a situation where their lives are shattered, or do you want to have financial security built up so they're fine?

If you're not in sales, building large amounts of passive income will likely take years. However, you don't necessarily need the massive amounts of time and money that I've had the benefit of having. Now, I say that because both time and money only amplify what's already there. And what's already there is your mindset and your skills, both of which you can improve to diversify your sources of cash inflow and build passive income.

Most of us have only worked 9 to 5 for the majority of our lives and only have one stream of income. There's nothing wrong with that, and if this is the life you're living now, it doesn't mean that things like passive income and financial security are off the table. They're not. Your life is the table, and you decide what goes on the table and what doesn't!

However, you need to know that if you want to build passive income and have financial security, you'll need to learn to think like those who've already achieved it in life. The fact of the matter is that most people aren't born with lots of money, and to make that money, they have to give time to what it is they do. What this means is that almost everyone in life, at some point, had neither time nor money, yet some of them managed to acquire both in abundance.

That said, you need to think of someone you know who's managed to achieve this in their life. It could be a famous celebrity, a friend, or a family member, and think about how they managed to achieve all that they did. The goal of this little exercise is not to mimic what they did in hopes of achieving the same results. This will help improve your mindset and give you a broader perspective on how to create multiple streams of passive income. Once you have certain ideas down, the rest of the journey will be pretty straightforward but filled with challenges.

Make no mistake, you'll need to learn and master new skills to truly diversify your income, and one of the most essential things you need to master is your money. Believe me when I tell you that both financial management and financial security are interlinked. You can't have one without the other. I say that because if you're in a position right now where you don't have multiple streams of income and financial security, you need to start managing your money better.

This is something that often starts with the good old-fashioned "cut back on your expenses" approach. This is what worked for me, and I'll tell you why. You see, if you only have one source of income, you can't really start a business (or a side hustle, for that matter) without some additional capital to diversify it. Cutting back on your expenses allows you to save up that money. After you have some additional cash saved, don't go for the business route right away.

Remember, financial security is about having enough money to deal with unexpected life events, and having financial security is more important than diversifying your income at first. This is what I was talking about earlier when I said the two are interlinked. You see, if you achieve financial security early on in life, you're free to invest the remaining amount of money or start a business with it.

However, if you don't have financial security, you'll always be at risk of disaster when you start a business or try to diversify your income. If you take the approach of not saving your money and using it to make more money, the financial risk you're exposed to greatly increases. In such a case, when you experience an adverse event, you put both your business or sources of additional income and your personal life at risk.

But the tables turn when you have diversified your income and have managed to earn it passively. At this stage, every single dollar you make contributes to your financial security. The more money you make, the more secure your personal and professional lives become. This also opens up more opportunities for you to make it big and live a million-dollar life! We'll talk more about this in the coming chapter. One thing I want you to take with you from all this is that financial security is highly important regardless of the stage of life you're in, and achieving it allows you to improve your financial position tenfold.

CHALLENGE |
THE POWER OF
FINANCIAL SECURITY

1. Who do you know who is financially stable, has a nice lifestyle, and does what they want?

2. What would happen to that person if they lost their main source of income? If they break their leg, their main business fails, etc., are they still financially set?

3. Who do you know who was financially set, had a life-altering event, and is no longer financially set?

4. What sources of income do you think you would want to diversify your income from?

CHAPTER 10

MILLION DOLLAR TRANSITION

"Without strategy, execution is aimless.
Without execution, strategy is useless."
— **Morris Chang**

Ah, college—the land of Ramen noodles and dreams. Back then, $100,000 wasn't just a number but the Holy Grail of success. I'd sit in my cramped dorm room, textbooks sprawled everywhere, and think, "Man, if I could just pull in a hundred grand a year, I'd be living the dream!" It seemed like the ultimate goal, my ticket to a life less ordinary. To me, hitting that six-figure salary was more than just a financial milestone; it was the neon-lit "You've Arrived" sign on the highway of life. If I could get there, I thought everything else would fall into place.

Oh man, then I found pest control—now that's where the stakes really started to rise. I made $30,000 my first summer, and I thought I was on top of the world; my second summer, I more than doubled that. I started listening to "Think and Grow Rich" and decided to make a 5-year plan. At the time, a $100,000 summer was the dream; it's what all the guys were going for. After building that 5-year plan, I decided to forget the $100,000 dream; that was kid stuff. Now, numbers like $200,000, $250,000, and even $500,000 started dancing in my head. Those sums seemed as outlandish as a Hollywood block-buster, but I couldn't shake them.

I left my then-current company because I realized I couldn't achieve my goals with their compensation plan, and I found greener pastures. My first summer at the new company, I made $180,000, and my second summer, I made $220,000. At that time, I made it; I had enough passive income to cover all my expenses. That was my goal for a few years now, so it was surreal when it finally happened. I took a step back and looked at my success. I started having more fun and wasting money. I joined a syndication and met guys who blew me out of the water, and then I realized I wanted more. I had the time; I had the resources, and I decided to redo my goals again and update my 5-year plan. Then came the big M—the million-dollar summer dream, the stuff of legend. And let me tell you, I wasn't just daydreaming about it; I was all in.

So, what did I do? I went full-on strategist, like a general plotting a battlefield. I laid out a five-year plan, breaking down every detail. We're talking teams, revenue goals, and even the tiniest of overrides that would lead me to that sweet seven-figure payday. It wasn't just about me hitting the jackpot; it was a team effort. My success was inextricably linked to theirs. I had to set them up for victory if I was going to hit my own grand slam. The mission? Make a million in one summer. Crazy? Maybe. Doable? Absolutely. And just like that, the hunt for the million was on.

The time I invested in this team was borderline obsessive. Think about it—I was grinding from 8 a.m. on Sundays straight through to 10 p.m. during the off-season. We're talking about a journey from zero sales reps from my time off for one year to having a small squad of 29 to a powerhouse of over 500 sales pros. The crazy part? I was all in on this gig without any immediate pay. My work in September and October was essentially an investment toward a paycheck I wouldn't cash until a year later. But the grind and hustle had a purpose—I knew that by summer, I could rake in a million dollars and build a team that would be my legacy.

Now, you might ask, how could I dive so deeply into something with a delayed payout? I've said it before, and it's worth repeating: asset diversification and solid systems made it possible. I put together a full lineup of people and tools to free up my time so I could focus my efforts where they count. I have Airbnb managers, a personal assistant, Turo car managers, and heck, even managers for those managers. Plus, I've got companies handling my Section 8 properties and accountants to keep the IRS happy. These aren't luxuries; they're essentials—systems that set the stage for my success.

These systems were crucial for setting myself up for success; otherwise, any wins would have been purely accidental. Without these systems, I'd be stuck in the weeds doing non-productive, active-income tasks like property maintenance and caring for my rental cars—tasks that would keep me from my million-dollar goal. Making the shift to delegate those responsibilities did hit my wallet at first, but it's a small price to pay because, let's be real, when you're shooting for massive growth, you need every second devoted to what's actually going to scale you up and blow you away.

My decision to go all-in with hyper-focus bucks conventional wisdom. You've likely heard the old adage: "Don't put all your eggs in one basket. Diversify. Create multiple streams of income." That's solid advice when you're just starting out or still learning the ropes of investing, and it's exactly what you need to do at the beginning. But once you're financially secure, you can afford to put all your new "eggs" into that one lucrative "basket"—especially if you have the financial know-how to manage risks effectively.

For me, now, that focus is on pest control; in the future, it'll shift to syndication. So, I constantly ask myself, How can I improve? How can I support my team better? How can I grow as a leader? And my intense focus has paid off. I've skyrocketed from a guy making $1.5 million in annual revenue to one pulling in $3 million, then $10 million, and now aiming for $30 million next year. This extreme, rapid growth is possible not just because I have the funds but also the time and energy to commit.

To truly live life on your own terms, there are two essential elements you need: income and time. This is the secret to making the million-dollar transition and reaching new heights in your endeavors. But how can you unlock this winning combination? Well, the first step is achieving financial security. Once you've accomplished that, a world of opportunities opens.

Those who have both a stable income and excellent credit gain access to a larger playing field. They can delve deeper into specialized investments and efficient workflows that not only generate more income but also free up valuable time. If you're already earning hundreds of thousands, you're on the right path. However, if you have the credit to support it, you can elevate your game further by leveraging other people's capital for smarter investments.

Looking back at the million-dollar transition, it was also a significant shift in mindset. My goal was not a million dollars before. But when I started improving and excelling, I upped my goals. I realized I needed to have higher goals because I was performing at a higher level.

Aiming for Your Million-Dollar Summer

So, if you want to aim for a million-dollar transition, you must not fear making that kind of leap. But above all, to achieve it, you must have the time and passive income, and you can't allow yourself to be derailed. It's incredibly easy to get sidetracked when things go awry—whether it's a property issue, legal matters, or any of life's unexpected challenges. Countless distractions can divert your attention.

What I've learned over the years is that maintaining a laser-like focus is something that's not as easy as it seems. Anyone can say that they're focusing on their goals, but I can tell you from experience that focusing on achieving the million-dollar transition is a completely different ball game altogether. One key thing I've picked up on is that our ability to think about what we can achieve greatly influences how "laser-sharp" our focus is. I've always felt that if you can see yourself achieving something in your head, then you'll be able to focus on it in real life.

This worked for me. Throughout my entire dorm life, I was thinking about the $100,000 payday, and that's why I was able to focus on that goal and achieve it in real life. I can tell you right now that this is exactly what you need to do, too. All of us have a finite amount of money and time in life, and this reality is embedded deep within our subconscious mind. However, to transition to the million-dollar life, you need to break free from this perceived reality.

Why, you ask? Well, thoughts like "I only have this much money" or "I only have so much time" place limitations on what we think we can achieve. This is something that'll make you lose before you even start. Placing limitations on what we think we can achieve greatly reduces the opportunities we believe are accessible to us and the ones we pursue. Stick with me for a second here.

Imagine you've just found out that starting a small-time software development company is a lucrative option. However, to pursue this venture, you need to have some knowledge of how software programs are developed. I'm not saying that you need to be a coder, but you still need enough knowledge to get your head around things so you can run the business. If you think something like, "I don't have that much time, I can't take a software or application development course, and I don't know anything about this industry." You're not going to get far.

You've placed a limitation on what you think you can achieve and will never pursue the opportunity. On the flip side, if you say to yourself, "I can take online courses over the weekend, maybe start as a freelancer, network with others to build my team, and go from there," you've just turned an idea into a viable plan that may very well be your million-dollar transition. Are you beginning to see the full picture here?

What I'm trying to say here is that you need to envision yourself doing what you would do if things like time and money weren't a factor. However, all this will only help you develop the focus you need. There's a lot more you'll need to do if you want to maintain that focus, and, make no mistake, you will need to maintain that focus. Life will always be filled with distractions, unexpected events, and the occasional "better option," but your ability to focus is what'll help you reach the million-dollar payday.

As far as things like uncertainty and failures are concerned, you need to have faith in what you're doing. Elon didn't give up after SpaceX's launch failures. You're no different, so why should you? As for the distractions, they'll be there, trying to get you off your game. To make sure they don't, you need to identify what's triggering them. There's always something that triggers a distraction, and you need to identify what that is.

Is it the environment? The place? The company you keep? A particular feeling or emotion? Make a note of whatever it is that triggers your distractions. Then work toward tackling the triggers, and your distraction will submit to you, not the other way around! Once you've done all this, you'll be in the right headspace to aim for the million-dollar transition.

CHALLENGE |
MILLION DOLLAR TRANSITION

1. If money weren't a factor, what major growth could you achieve?

2. What amount of money would you need to make to become financially fearless?

3. If time weren't a factor, where would you put the majority of your time?

4. What is your plan to become financially fearless?

5. Who can you think of who is financially fearless?

6. What examples can you think of where, if the person weren't financially fearless, they would have failed?

CHAPTER 11

UNDERSTANDING ASSETS AND LIABILITIES

*The key is to work extremely hard for a short period of time
(1-5 years), create abundant wealth, and then make money
work hard for you through wise investments that yield a passive
income for life.*
—**H.W. Charles**

Let's shake up your understanding of assets and liabilities. If you think you've got it all figured out, hang tight—your existing ideas might be flawed and could set up roadblocks on your journey to financial freedom.

Now, most people have a basic grasp of assets and liabilities. You own a house; it's an asset, right? After all, that's what school and society tell us: go get a loan for a car after school; it will be an asset by getting you around places; buy a house and get a mortgage; it will be the biggest asset in your life and be your nest egg. Not so fast. Financial guru Robert Kiyosaki is famous for declaring that your home is not an asset but a liability because it consistently drains your wallet for repairs, maintenance, and taxes.

My wife was in school and had a class that was talking about finances; one of the questions was, "Is a house a liability or an asset?" Since I had read a lot of Kiyosaki's books, I instantly said it was a liability. She got the question wrong: How can people be at such odds? It's because it's not broken down enough.

There are two sides of assets and two sides of liabilities. Sorry, Robert, but I'd like to throw my own hat into the ring. In my view, if something appreciates in value, it is an asset; if it drains your pockets at a slower rate than it appreciates, then it is a cash-sucking asset. For example, if someone bought a house in 2019 and didn't fill it with tenants and you're having to pay the $3K mortgage every month, you could see Robert's point that it's a liability. However, if you sold that house in 2022 for a $100K profit, then it's obvious that the schools were right.

Real estate is a perfect example of how this can pan out. You may own property that seems to suck money out of you for ongoing maintenance, making it feel like a "cash-draining asset." But if its market value is rising, you're still in the green in the long term. On the flip side, you can get a property that is producing you cash and is appreciating; maybe you're renting out rooms in your house; maybe you got a property whose rents cover the mortgage and make a profit. This is a cash-producing asset; everyone wants to find cash-producing assets because it seems like the most logical way to become financially secure. You'll notice that most major businesses are cash-draining assets; once you become financially secure, you'll most likely find the greatest returns by turning off instant gratification.

A car can be a cash-draining liability, or it could be a cash-producing liability. Have you ever thought about your car in this context? Say you own a car that you rent out. It's generating money, but it's also depreciating—so what is it? In my book, it's a "cash-producing liability," and understanding these categories can be game-changing for your financial strategy.

Assets and liabilities aren't inherently good or bad; it's all about how you manage them and where you are in your life. Having a Ferrari might seem like a significant liability, but if you're in an industry where you need to attract or recruit people, it could be a tremendous asset because it's bringing you more value than you're losing with the depreciation.

Donald Trump made a great addition to this point; he talked about someone who was financially broke and restarting from a failed business. Even though he was struggling financially, he would always fly first class. It might have seemed like a waste of money, but it helped boost his ego so much that he would attend business meetings on a high rather than having had the poor experience he could have had on a low-level airline flying economy.

In 2008, the housing market crashed, and people owed more on their houses than they were worth; these cash-draining assets just turned into cash-draining liabilities. That was a white swan event that wasn't predictable, so don't base your financial decisions solely on these events that aren't predictable (COVID, a hurricane, stock market collapse), but make sure to diversify your assets and liabilities so your entire financial security doesn't come crashing down at once.

What you need to avoid at all costs are cash-draining liabilities; buying a car with a high payment for no reason; it doesn't help you in any way; you don't need it to recruit; you don't need it for your job; you just got it because it seemed like a cool idea. Maybe you inherit a house—a presumed asset—but if you mismanage it or it needs so much work that it won't increase in value by the amount you have to maintain and fix it, you could find yourself swimming in debt, possibly losing the property.

To simplify, I categorize investments into four buckets.

1. Cash-producing assets: These increase in value and also generate income.

2. Cash-Draining Assets: These appreciate in value but require ongoing financial upkeep.

3. Cash-Producing Liabilities: These are depreciating but also generate income.

4. Cash-Draining Liabilities: These neither appreciate nor generate income and require financial upkeep.

The crux of the matter is answering two questions: "Is it appreciating in value or bringing me more value?" and "Is it generating income?" The answers will help you understand the true nature of your investments.

What if you could retire purely on liabilities? Imagine if the income from a bunch of depreciating cars covered your $5,000 monthly expenses. Traditionally, they're liabilities, but if they're fulfilling your financial needs, that's a game-changer.

And yes, there are always exceptions. Like a stock that doesn't appreciate but pays dividends—it's still an asset. Cash, often seen as an asset, can actually be a liability due to the silent creep of inflation, which diminishes its value.

Now that you have a better idea of assets and liabilities, I'm going to destroy your understanding again! Just kidding, but I want to expand and plant some ideas in your head. Some people will look at this book and decide they're SOL; they're trapped under tons of debt; they stink at sales; don't have time, etc. Or maybe you're a college student who doesn't want to go knock on doors with me and make hundreds of thousands of dollars. You might think that you won't be able to get assets, but you already have tons of assets! You also have tons of liabilities.

You have assets in that there are things you're good at, things that you can continue to develop and market. Maybe you're great at the cello; maybe you're great at coding; go train others to be great at it; go make courses and sell the courses. You have assets that aren't tangible; tap into them and use them.

This book isn't as much about mental liabilities, but they're out there, and they're real. Maybe it's a nagging voice; maybe it's trauma from a parent always shooting your ideas down and mentally beating you into submission. Go read "Pluck the FUD" by Ben Ward; this will help you identify your mental liabilities and how to pluck them out.

The idea here is to look at yourself in terms of assets and liabilities and classify all that you have into the four buckets I mentioned earlier. If this seems a bit overwhelming to you, worry not. I'll help you out. The very first thing that you need to do is make a list of all the skills you have and all the liabilities that are keeping you down. Understand that all of your skills will go into the asset buckets, and everything that keeps you down will go into the liability buckets.

The real fun begins once you have all this mapped, so I recommend that you take a piece of paper and a pen (you don't need a No.2 pencil) and write everything down in the four categories. If you're thinking, "What am I going to do after that?"Then sit tight; we're going to cover that in detail. The key to using this approach to manage your assets and liabilities and leveraging them for success is time and money. Yes, we're back to time and money again. Allow me to explain.

You see, both time and money are for you what water is to plant. When you've categorized skills and drawbacks as assets and liabilities in the four buckets, you'll see that the first one will contain your top skills. These are skills that will be valuable in the future, and you can make money from them right now. It could be anything. If you're a musician, you could play small-time gigs at local cafes for some extra cash, and who knows, maybe one day you'll be even more successful than the Beatles. If you're into AI and coding, maybe you can find some freelance work online, and in the future, you could be the one who bridges the gap between AI and human consciousness.

Whatever is in bucket number one is what you need to use to make money now and nurture it, so it will be of greater value later. This is where you need to dedicate the maximum amount of time and money.

Now, onto bucket number two. These are things that are generating money, but they require some upkeep. I'm not going to bore you to death with another example here; I'm going to cut right to the chase. You still need to focus on these skills because they'll be valuable in the future, but you need to figure out a way of how you're going to dump all of this into bucket number one. This means that you need to figure out how you can use what's in bucket number two to make money now. You'll still dedicate time and money to bucket number two, but not as much as you will for the first one.

Bucket number three will contain most of what's keeping you down and will cause your value to depreciate, but it is doing you some good right now. You don't want to dedicate too much time or money to these things, but you should milk them for what they have to offer.

As for bucket number four, these are things that won't do you any good, aren't doing you any good, and are keeping you down. Make no mistake; these are the anchors you need to cut loose. There's absolutely no need to dedicate any time to whatever's in this bucket. Get rid of it as soon as you can.

Once you've mastered using this approach for all that you are right now, turn things up a notch. Actively look for cash-producing assets and cash-producing liabilities. These are things that will either go up or down in value in the future but will always generate income in the present moment. List down what these things are for you and plan how you'll acquire them and use them to your benefit.

Manage your assets and liabilities like this, and your life's balance sheet will be in good shape!

CHALLENGE |
UNDERSTANDING ASSETS
AND LIABILITIES

1. What was your understanding of an asset, and how has it changed?

2. What was your understanding of a liability, and how has it changed?

3. What examples of cash-draining assets have you seen and could have made tons of money on?

4. What are some liabilities that you're now realizing could be cash-producing?

5. What cash-producing assets or cash-producing liabilities can you acquire right now? And how much would you need to cover your expenses?

6. What is your plan to obtain these cash-producing assets, liabilities, and cash-draining liabilities?

7. What cash-sucking liabilities do you need to cut from your life, and when will you cut them?

CHAPTER 12
NAVIGATING FINANCIAL OBSTACLES

"You gain strength, courage, and confidence by every experience in which you really stop to look fear in the face. You must do the thing you think you cannot do."
—Eleanor Roosevelt

There is a common problem that many people face when working on acquiring assets. They look at financing as a black-and-white endeavor. They like to see things as status quo; there's only one way to play the financing game. "This is how we're not supposed to do it." They don't understand that there are many gray areas when it comes to creatively financing their projects. They aren't aware of legitimate loopholes or how to discover and implement them.

When I was 22, I made $180,000, blew all of it, and ended up filing for bankruptcy. This put a huge wrench in my financial planning. My game plan was to acquire a set number of properties every year and retire by the age of 25.

After my bankruptcy, I assumed I couldn't acquire real estate assets because I had ruined my credit. I thought I could do nothing except make some hard cash offers on assets, but that wasn't very attractive. However, when I made $200,000 the second year, I realized that I had a misconception about financing real estate. You don't have to rely on your own credit; you can also leverage other people's credit. I started doing a lot of research and discovered owner financing, where I could find people who were willing to sell me their properties and act as the bank.

I also discovered ways to get other people to take out loans using their credit and my money for the down payment on the property. I had to get super scrappy and navigate the gray areas to continue accomplishing my goals and aim for retirement.

Now, some loopholes will help you in these kinds of situations. One big loophole is that reported income is a myth when you're on a

1099. You can report as much or as little as you want, depending on which expenses you apply against your income. There are some very tricky ways to get around this.

For example, having an LLC in New Mexico or Wyoming is a great way to conceal your identity. Banks can't see where the money is coming from other than as a business. They can't see that you're the owner. So, you set it up so that your New Mexico or Wyoming LLC pays you a 1099 income. This makes it a lot easier to get loans if you have a consistent 1099 income.

One of the best things to do in this situation is to start building credit backups with Experian Boost. Get credit cards you'll be able to make payments on and keep your balances very low, as that will quickly boost your credit. The big loophole, if you have bad credit, is to use other people's credit. That's fine; you don't need to have good credit yourself.

If you have a bad debt-to-income ratio, that's where the real loopholes can get more complex. When I first got married, I made my wife the owner of some new businesses and had her W-2 me because we had different last names. I had an LLC in Utah that was paying me, as I didn't yet know about the privacy advantages of New Mexico or Wyoming LLCs.

Creating a 1099 income for yourself is one of the best ways to improve your financial standing. If you have Airbnb income, most banks and financial institutions won't count that income towards your debt-to-income ratio, so you have to get creative. If you have an Airbnb that consistently brings in over $2,000 a month, create an LLC in New Mexico or Wyoming and have the Airbnb pay that business instead of you. Then, set up a property lease agreement between you and the LLC, and have the LLC pay you $2,000 a month and give you a 1099 at the end of the tax year. As long as you have two years of 1099 income, in most cases, this income will count toward helping you qualify for a loan.

You can apply this same strategy to a Turo business. Create a Turo LLC business that's getting paid from renting cars, and then create leases for the cars for the business. This will give you consistent income every month, making it easier for banks to approve loans because they see you're receiving consistent payments from a business.

By setting up these private LLCs and paying yourself monthly, you raise your debt-to-income ratio, which helps you qualify for more financing.

Another obstacle you'll likely face is that your credit history won't be long enough to get certain loans. To solve this, circle back and consider implementing the credit-building strategies I mentioned earlier in the book. Remember when we talked about things like getting a secured credit card and those store-branded credit cards? We even went into detail about how you can ask a friend or a family member with a good credit history to help you out. You can ask to be listed as an authorized user on their credit cards. This neat little trick will allow their credit to give yours a nice little piggyback ride, but this is something that you should rush. You need to make sure that the person you choose has a good credit history.

Believe me when I say that there will be a few times in life when you'll need financing options. Acquiring cash-producing assets and liabilities might be one. Truth be told, if you just stick back and save until the day you have enough to acquire some cash-producing assets and liabilities, you won't have enough. You'll probably miss out on some lucrative opportunities, too, because someone somewhere is going to beat you to the chase. To make sure that doesn't happen, you'll need to avail yourself of financing options, and this will be a smooth ride for you if you have good credit.

And now, the big one: debt! It's no secret that debt is one of the biggest financial obstacles you'll face in life. Most financial books, videos, and blogs you'll find online will tell you to use either the snowball or the avalanche approach to clear your debt, but what I like to do is combine the two. You see, with the snowball method, you start by paying off your smallest debt first and work your way up to the largest one. Whereas with the avalanche one, you start by paying off the one with the highest interest first and then work your way down.

So, you choose a method and make minimum contributions to all your debts. After that, whatever excess cash you have is to be used to pay off the smallest one or the one with the highest interest, depending on the method you choose. But what I like to do is combine both of these approaches. I start with the snowball method because it helps give me momentum, and when I feel I'm in the groove, I switch over to the avalanche one. That's exactly what you need to do, too. The snowball method will give you the discipline you need, and the avalanche method will take care of those high-interest debts.

Before we go into evaluating your income, I would urge you to identify the financial obstacles in your life and use what you've learned to plan how you'll navigate them!

CHALLENGE |
NAVIGATING FINANCIAL OBSTACLES

1. Take a moment to identify one misconception you've held about financing assets. How can you start exploring creative financing options?

2. What's your game plan for acquiring assets? Whether you're recovering from a financial setback or just getting started, set a clear goal for the next year and outline a step-by-step plan to achieve it.

3. Do you have bad credit or a challenging debt-to-income ratio? Explore at least one of the mentioned loopholes that can help you improve your financing options. Take the first step today.

4. Consider your own financial privacy. Are there ways you can enhance it, like setting up an LLC in a specific state? Investigate the options available in your area.

5. Building your credit history is crucial. Which of the credit-building strategies mentioned in the chapter resonates with you the most? Commit to implementing it and monitor your progress over the next six months.

CHAPTER 13
EVALUATING INCOME STREAMS

"Don't just visualize success at the end. Visualize the process. Don't just picture yourself winning. Picture the steps it takes to get there."
—Dean Bokhari

et's dive deeper into different income types, using case studies and practical examples to showcase the power of passive income. While most of my examples feature salesmen and managers I've worked with—individuals earning substantial amounts—it's important to remember that high income alone doesn't guarantee financial freedom.

Your task: Read through the following examples carefully. For each case, identify which financial quadrant the individual falls into and consider what steps they could take to bolster their financial security.

AARON

Meet Aaron, a 20-year-old who wears many hats. He flips cars, works as a professional car broker, and shines as a high-level recruiter and salesman. First off, let's delve into his skill set. Aaron is no one-trick pony; he knows his way around the car market and can broker deals and buy and resell cars on a smaller scale. When it comes to recruitment, the guy is a star—an absolute ace. Sales? He's got that covered, too.

Now, let's pivot to his financial landscape. Aaron is juggling $6,000 in monthly expenses. At first glance, it looks like he has no passive income, but hold on—a $700 monthly inflow comes from a pair of rental properties he owns. On paper, he's got a net worth that includes $500,000 in assets. However, there's also a $190,000 cloud of liabilities looming overhead, mostly in the form of $180,000 in loans. Do the math, and you'll find that if Aaron were to settle his debts and liquidate his assets, he'd be sitting on a cool $310,000. Without those loan payments, his monthly expenses could shrink to a more manageable $2,000 to $2,500 range.

But here's the snag: Aaron's assets are, for the most part, tied up. He can't sell or trade them; they're essentially stuck in financial limbo. They're not liquid and are best described as "hard assets."

So, what's next for Aaron? What quadrant does he currently reside in, and what steps does he need to take to graduate to the next level? The hiccup in his asset game is that each piece of his property portfolio needs a cash injection of around $10,000 to $20,000 for upgrades or repairs. That's actually where some of his existing debt originates. Until those issues are resolved, he's more or less stuck in his current financial position, particularly because he's cash-poor.

His endgame? Aaron aims to rake in $250,000 per year through passive income. So, the question is: What actionable steps should he consider to turn his financial ship around?

EVAN

Meet Evan, a dynamo in the worlds of recruitment, sales, and management. This guy isn't just dabbling; he's crafting systems and processes that make him a true standout. Yet, despite his knack for creating income avenues, he's a bit strapped for cash. Why? While he's not closing sales left and right, he's built an impressive pipeline that's set to pump about $100,000 his way.

Let's not forget Evan's a multitasker—juggling college life while also having a side hustle with his car. Yep, he leases it out to a friend, so there's a small but steady cash flow there. The financial horizon looks promising, too. He's eyeing a windfall of around $200,000 in about four to six months. His only financial anchors are his college fees and rent, which keep his liabilities to a minimum.

So, what's the verdict on Evan's current financial landscape? It's a high-risk, high-reward game he's playing. He's low on immediate funds but stands to rake in a significant sum in the near future.

What's next on the docket for Evan? Immediate cash flow is a concern, so nailing down some quick sales could bridge the gap until that pipeline starts delivering. Given that he's not drowning in monthly expenses, now is the time to focus on shorter sales cycles or look for other side gigs that can bring in instant cash.

There you have it—the financial snapshot of Evan and the fork in the road he's facing. What actionable steps should this young go-getter consider to keep the ship sailing smoothly?

PAUL

Step into the world of Paul, a guy who's basically the LeBron James of his fields. This guy isn't just smart; he's a genius—he scored a 35 on the ACT if you need proof. Paul is a highest-level salesman—top in the industry, no less. He's the highest-level recruiter and a high-level manager. When it comes to earnings, we're talking between $500,000 and a million bucks every year. Yeah, he's not buying islands, but he's not pinching pennies, either.

With that kind of dough, Paul's got the freedom to live life in style. He owns a swanky house that he's invested a pretty penny in, decking it out like a page from a luxury magazine. But let's pause for a second—other than his real estate play, he doesn't have any other assets. Passive income? Zero, zip, nada. Yet, thanks to his robust earnings, he's kept his debt-to-income ratio in the safe zone. How? By paying cash for nearly everything.

So, where's Paul on the financial quadrant map? He's banking on active income with no passive streams to diversify his portfolio. The guy's got skills that pay the bills, but what if he ever decides to hang up his salesman shoes? He'd be missing a financial safety net.

What's next for this high roller? Paul needs to think long-term. Diversification is the name of the game. With his skills, perhaps branching into mentorship or consulting could add another revenue stream. Have you ever thought about real estate investments that could generate passive income? He's already got a taste for properties, so why not take it to the next level?

Bottom line: Paul's got skills and earnings to envy, but there's room to grow. He's got to consider ways to future-proof his financial landscape. So, what are the must-do action items for Paul to level up from here?

FAITH

Meet Faith, the triple-threat dynamo in the world of music, teaching, and business. You've got to hear this: She's a high-level piano player and one of the industry's top violin performers. But she's not just about performing; she's also a top-notch educator, raking in about $100 an hour teaching violin. Hold up; there's more—she's got an MLM business, too, flexing her high-level leadership and visionary skills, which pad her wallet with a few extra grand each month. Did I mention she's got a killer business mind on top of all that?

Now, with her diverse skill set and income streams, Faith's not just a one-hit wonder. She's got a stable and diverse cash flow, blending her artistic talents with her entrepreneurial prowess. The MLM angle throws a bit of passive income into the mix, and her teaching gigs are like a fine-tuned machine that keeps churning out the bucks.

So, where does Faith land in the financial quadrant? She's got her hands in multiple pots—active income from her teaching and performances and passive income from her MLM business. She's a blend of talent and hustle, making her well-positioned to scale her income further if she wants to.

What's next in line for this multi-talented maestro? With her business acumen, she might want to consider expanding her brand. Online courses? Merch? A high-end consulting service for up-and-coming musicians or MLM enthusiasts? The sky's the limit for someone with her skills and ambition.

Bottom line: Faith's killing it on multiple fronts. She's got the talent, the business chops, and the diversified income to prove it. So, what's on the to-do list for Faith to level up from here?

HOPE

Get ready to meet Hope, a high-level violin player, teacher, and networker who's totally acing the game of life. She's not just hustling; she's raking in around $10,000 a month in passive income—think properties and MLM action. And let's not forget, she's got a supportive husband with a steady paycheck and a growing family of little virtuosos.

Financially speaking, Hope's got the kind of setup most people daydream about. Her monthly expenses of $8,000? Covered, with room to spare. So, in the world of financial quadrants, Hope is living in that coveted spot where passive income outweighs expenses. She's in a comfortable zone, but the lady's got room to level up.

What's the next power move for Hope? She's already got a lot going for her, so the question is about scaling. Maybe it's time to reinvest that extra monthly income into more properties or level up in her MLM gig. And hey, with her networking skills, creating a professional community or offering high-end courses could be her next golden ticket.

But let's not forget the family dynamics. With multiple kids and a husband bringing in steady cash, Hope may want to aim for financial growth and more family time. So, finding ventures that require less day-to-day management could be a win-win. Think about ventures that bring both cash and time—time she can spend with her family or even practicing that high-level violin skill.

Bottom line: Hope's already got a well-oiled financial machine. Now, she's got to decide how to fine-tune it for even more gains and maybe some extra family jams. So, what are Hope's next best steps for leveling up?

DANIEL

Oh boy, Daniel's in a tight spot, huh? High-level salesman? Check. Motivated? Absolutely. But let's get real—this guy's financial IQ needs a makeover, like yesterday. I can't pay rent because commissions are slow. That's a red flag. Add to that an ex-girlfriend who's pregnant, owes money left and right, and has zero assets. Man, Daniel's playing life on hard mode.

So, where is he in the financial quadrant? In a tough spot—that's where. He's wholly dependent on active income, and even that's not working out for him. If nothing changes, Daniel's on a fast track to financial ruin and serious personal stress.

First things first, Daniel's got to get his cash flow sorted. If commissions aren't cutting it, he needs a short-term solution. It's a side gig, perhaps? Selling some stuff? He's a high-level salesman; surely, he can close some quick deals. He also needs to negotiate with the people he owes money to—getting on some payment plan or something.

Next up is budgeting. This guy needs to know where every penny's going and why. We're talking about basic personal finance hygiene here. Maybe get a financial advisor on board—someone to give him the 411 on managing money.

Now, what got Daniel into this mess? Procrastination and poor money management are big culprits. Also, maybe he's been focusing on the short term—chasing commissions—without thinking of long-term stability. And hey, life threw him a curveball with the pregnancy news, which makes sorting his finances even more urgent.

Daniel needs a complete overhaul—a step-by-step action plan that takes him from financial zero to hero. He's already got the motivation; now he needs the plan and the discipline to stick to it. If he doesn't change his ways, the future's not looking too bright. Time to hustle, Daniel.

BRIAN

Alright, meet Brian. This guy's basically a Swiss Army knife of skills—top-notch recruiter, killer manager, pro salesman—and even knows his way around some code. On paper, this dude's crushing it. But here's the kicker: he's got revenue in the millions, yet almost no profit to show for it, thanks to some massive liabilities. And let's talk about that Tesla Model Plaid. Braden's monthly payment is $2,000, and Tesla just went ahead and dropped the price on him. Ouch.

Financially speaking, the guy is in hot water. No passive income streams and just enough to cover basic expenses for a year? Plus, he's got two kids at home, one of whom is a newborn. So, in terms of financial quadrants, he's stuck between being self-employed and a business owner, but without the perks of either.

If Brian doesn't make drastic changes, his financial roller coaster will crash. And don't forget, his time is already stretched thin. He needs those teams to function, or his payday could turn into a pay-no-way.

So, what's the game plan? First, he must find a way to lower those liabilities. That could mean restructuring debt or renegotiating contracts. Whatever it takes to make that revenue actually turn into profit

Next is the Tesla. He's upside-down on the car loan, which is bad news, bears. It might be time to consider selling it at a loss and getting something more economical, especially with a growing family.

On the passive income front, Braden needs to think long-term. Given his time constraints, he might look into low-maintenance investment options, like index funds or real estate, where a property manager handles the day-to-day. Even though it might not bring immediate cash flow, it's a start for financial freedom.

And finally, he's got to find a way to delegate more responsibilities. He can't be the linchpin for everything, especially with two kids now. Hiring an operations manager could free up some of his time, which he can then invest in ventures that can bring in some much-needed passive income.

Bottom line: Brian's in a financial crunch, but not dead-end. It's time to switch gears and rethink his game plan, or he's risking a major financial fumble.

MARK

Mark is a high-level salesman but a pretty poor manager with low motivation. He's been in the sales game for a while and was on track to make $150,000 this year. Unfortunately, one of his teams dropped the ball, and now he's looking at maybe $60,000 to $70,000. He's already spent most of it and hasn't managed his money well. On top of that, he's got an alcohol issue that's draining him emotionally and financially. He's leasing a car for $1,200 monthly and has only $2,000 in the bank. Feeling burned out, Mark is also facing a lease that is ending in two months, right when rents are expected to rise and the sales season will have ended.

What do you think Mark should have done differently to not be in this position? What quadrant is he in right now? What immediate action items should he take? What will happen to him if he doesn't change anything?

DAVID

David is a solid salesman and a manager who is not top-tier but knows his way around. He's also a college student, which adds another layer to his life. Over the summer, he raked in over $100,000 selling pest control and has big ambitions. He wants to recruit massive teams so he can really ramp up his investments. I just picked up a Corvette with a $1,000-a-month payment. He's got some assets, too, like a share in a cabin through the Syndicate Project. With about $40,000 sitting in the bank, David's is in a unique spot for a college kid. So, what quadrant is David in? What should he be focusing on right now? There are some risks in his current setup—what steps should he take to level up?

The overarching story here is the importance of diversifying income streams and responsibly managing assets and liabilities for long-term financial security. Each individual brings their own set of strengths and challenges to the table, allowing us to explore a range of financial situations and solutions.

Aaron's situation demonstrates the pitfalls of tying up assets and taking on too much debt, leaving him cash-poor. Evan, despite his potential, lacks immediate cash flow, highlighting the importance of having multiple revenue streams to bridge financial gaps. Paul, while extremely successful in earning, lacks passive income, putting his financial stability at risk if he were to stop working. Faith exemplifies how diverse skill sets can help in building both active and passive income streams, making her well-poised for financial growth. Hope's life showcases the benefits of passive income exceeding expenses but questions how to leverage her situation for even greater financial and personal gains. Daniel's case is a cautionary tale of poor financial management and planning, emphasizing the urgent need for financial literacy and immediate action. Brian, despite a seemingly successful exterior, suffers from poor financial choices that threaten to collapse his empire.

These profiles form a vivid mirror of what to do—and what not to do—to achieve financial freedom and security. They underscore the importance of balancing different income types, managing liabilities, and focusing on both immediate and future financial needs. So, what's the next step for you? Are you Aaron, trying to unlock your hard assets? Paul, sitting comfortably but unprepared for a rainy day? Or perhaps Daniel is in dire need of a financial overhaul?

Identify your financial archetype, learn from their successes and pitfalls, and take decisive action to pivot your story towards a financially secure future. It's never too late to make the switch and adapt strategies that protect you and propel you forward. Act now, and don't let the lessons from Aaron to Brian go to waste. Take control of your financial destiny.

CHAPTER 14
PASSIVE INCOME MINDSET

Now that you've journeyed through the stories of Aaron, Evan, Paul, Faith, Hope, Daniel, and Brian, it's time to shift gears. Throughout the book, we have talked about strategy, diversification, and risk management, but remember, all the financial know-how in the world is useless without the right mindset.

You have the power to write your own financial story, but like an Olympic athlete in training, it requires a laser-sharp focus on your goals. You've gained the tools and the wisdom; now it's about setting your daily intentions, auditing your time, evaluating your relationships, and always—always—keeping your eyes on the prize: achieving unchained wealth through passive income.

Ready to get started? Let's lock in that mindset and sprint towards the finish line.

Start Your Day with Intention

Begin each morning by reviewing your daily goals in alignment with your passive income ambitions. For instance, you could start your day by reading an article on real estate investments or by monitoring stock market trends. The point is to set your mind on achieving passive income right from the get-go.

Time Audit

Conduct a 'Time Audit' by jotting down how you spend each hour. Are you sinking time into Netflix binges or aimlessly scrolling social media? Redirect that time into activities like researching potential investments or taking an online finance course. Treat it like an athlete treats their training schedule, with rigorous intentionality.

Evaluate and Adjust Your Inner Circle

Just as athletes have coaches and teammates that uplift them, your circle should do the same. If your closest friends are big spenders who scoff at the idea of investing, maybe it's time to start networking at investment seminars or joining online financial communities. The idea is to surround yourself with people who share your vision for passive income.

Review and Adjust

End your day or week by revisiting your to-do list and finance logs. Did you stray from your budget? Did you miss a potentially lucrative investment opportunity? Learn from these moments, like when an athlete reviews game tape, and adjust your plan for the next day or week accordingly.

Responsible Spending

Before making a purchase, ask yourself, "Is this a want or a need?" Just as an athlete wouldn't down a soda before a big race, avoid spontaneous splurges that can set back your financial progress. Opt for investments or experiences that contribute to your long-term financial health.

Learning from Coaches and Mentors

Whether it's a podcast from a successful entrepreneur or advice from a financially savvy family member, lean on these "coaches" for tips and motivation. They've been where you are and can provide roadmaps to where you want to go.

Daily Habits

Commit to daily habits that inch you closer to your passive income goals. For example, spend 20 minutes every day reading financial news or make it a routine to set aside 10% of your daily earnings into a separate investment account. View these activities as your daily training drills that prepare you for the financial marathons ahead.

Achieving a sustainable passive income is a marathon, not a sprint. It demands razor-sharp focus, disciplined routines, and an unwavering commitment to your financial future. Like an Olympic athlete, make every choice, every habit, and every association count toward your ambitions for passive income and financial freedom.

Your health is your most valuable asset, so invest in it wisely. Prioritize balanced eating to fuel your body; think of it as premium fuel for a high-performance vehicle. Don't skimp on sleep; restorative rest prepares your mind for the strategic thinking and decision-making you'll need. Incorporate regular physical activity into your routine, even if it's just a daily walk.

Finally, quality time with family and loved ones shouldn't be neglected. Just as a team provides emotional and psychological support for an athlete, your family is your emotional grounding, offering a mental respite from the rigors of financial strategizing.

RESULTS SPEAK

How will you know if your passive income mindset is on point? Look no further than the results of your life. Financial milestones will be reached, and your asset columns will grow, yes, but there's more to it than just numbers on a spreadsheet. Your body will feel energized, not drained; your close relationships will deepen in quality, not just exist out of habit.

Your life becomes a reflection of your mindset, a tangible scorecard of your focus, discipline, and decision-making. If you're not liking what you see, it's an opportunity for self-reflection and adjustment. So pay close attention to both your bank account and your life account. Both should be in excellent shape if you're truly living the passive income mindset.

CHAPTER 15
UNCHAINED WEALTH

"Expect the best. Prepare for the worst.
Capitalize on what comes."
—Zig Ziglar

As we wrap up this book, let's get that fire burning inside you.

You're young and in sales, and you know the adrenaline surge of closing deals and hitting targets. But forget quotas for a second. The most critical deal you'll ever close is with yourself—to live a life of unchained wealth. What's your freedom quota? How free and boundless do you want your lifestyle to be?

This isn't about dreaming; it's about waking up to a life you designed, not one designed for you. Imagine mornings without blaring alarms, only waking up because you're rested and ready. No mandatory meetings, no reports due, just the joy of seizing the day. However, you damn well please. Whether that's jet-setting to a tropical island on a whim, enjoying an afternoon drive in your dream car, or making it to every one of your kid's soccer games down the road—you call the shots.

Imagine a life without the cycle of bills and debt, replacing financial anxieties with choices, opportunities, and freedom. Unchained wealth isn't just about having money; it's about having options, time, and resources. It's about a life lived on your terms, a life full of limitless potential and peace of mind, where your wildest dreams aren't just possible—they're your reality.

Unchained wealth isn't just freedom from debt or the freedom to buy cool stuff. It's the freedom to live. To take the shot without worrying about missing. To invest in your dreams without the fear of failing. To give your loved ones not just a better life but the best life. Imagine never having to miss a family event, never having to say, "Sorry, I can't make it; I've got work." Instead, you're saying, "Where and when? I'm there." That's the difference between living for a paycheck and living for a purpose.

Here's the kicker: Unchained Wealth is not just about cold, hard cash—it's about the richness of choice, the richness of time, and the richness of spirit. Your 20s are the foundation of your financial future. The moves you make now can fast-track you to a life where you're not just existing but thriving. No boundaries, no limits—just limitless potential.

And let's talk about confidence because when you're financially unchained, confidence isn't just a state of mind; it's your way of life. You walk into rooms differently. You negotiate differently. Hell, you even flirt differently! Why? Because you've got the ultimate trump card: the freedom to walk away from anything that doesn't serve you. From toxic jobs to toxic relationships, you have the financial and emotional freedom to say, "I deserve better," and pursue exactly that.

Forget about hitting your sales targets for a moment. What's the target for your life? Imagine waking up not to a buzzing alarm but to the realization that you get to decide how to spend each moment of your day. No more nine-to-five, no more forced smiles at dull company mixers—just pure, unadulterated freedom. That's the dream, right? But how do we get there?

Remember the four degrees of financial freedom? Those are your steps to the life you want.

1. **Financially Set**: Here, your basics are covered. The bills are paid, and you're not losing sleep over sudden expenses.

2. **Financially Free**: Now, you're not just surviving—you're thriving. This is the point where your assets start to build up, and your debts are largely a thing of the past.

3. **Financially Secure**: At this level, you've got a good handle on your investments and cash flow. Your money works for you, not the other way around.

4. **Financially Fearless**: Here, you're practically unstoppable. Your wealth isn't just a safety net—it's a launchpad for whatever dreams you might conceive.

Always keep this in mind: Your credit score is like an invisible hand shaping your financial destiny. Whether it's getting approved for a mortgage or negotiating interest rates, that three-digit number plays a crucial role. So, give it the attention it deserves!

We also talked about the four quadrants of money. Depending on your income and credit situation, you'll fall into one of these categories:

High Income, High Credit

High Income, Low Credit

Low Income, High Credit

Low Income, Low Credit

Knowing where you stand helps you focus your efforts more effectively.

You can't build unchained wealth without financial literacy. Know how to read a balance sheet, understand the stock market, and get a grip on tax laws. It's like knowing the rules of the game so you can play to win.

Finally, we come to income-producing assets, the final piece of the puzzle. Once your money starts making more money, that's when you truly become financially free.

This is your moment, so don't just close this book and put it on a shelf. Use it as a playbook to change the game. Your game. Because, let's face it, you're not in your 20s forever. The actions you take today can catapult you into a life you've only daydreamed about. And time? Well, time is ticking. But the good news is that the balls are in your court.

Be bold and live unchained from the shackles of limited income that come with a traditional career. As you venture out into the world, remember this: You have the drive and the tools to make unchained wealth a reality. This isn't just for someone else; it's for you. So, no more excuses. No more 'somedays.' Today is the day. Your future is waiting, and it's one hell of a bright one.

Now go out there and light it up. Because a life of Unchained Wealth isn't just a dream; for you, it's a destiny. And destiny waits for no one. Seize it. Own it. Live it.

ACKNOWLEDGMENTS

Writing a book is a journey that one never truly takes alone, and this one is no exception. I would like to take a moment to express my deepest gratitude to the incredible people who have helped bring this dream to life.

First and foremost, I'd like to extend my thanks to David Strauss. Your guidance as my writing coach and editor has made this book possible. Your expertise and wisdom have not only shaped this book but have also expanded my reach by inspiring my sales teams.

To my beautiful wife, you are the cornerstone of my world. Your unwavering support and love have been my constant source of inspiration and strength. You make every challenge easier and every victory sweeter. You have always supported me and pushed me to hit my goals.

My parents, thank you for giving me life and instilling in me an entrepreneurial mindset.

My brother Joseph, thank you for believing in me enough to co-sign on my first two properties.

To my sisters, Hope and Charity, incredible thanks for helping us through the most difficult time of our lives.

To the rest of my family, thank you for your continued support.

Ben Ward, your insights and teachings have paved the way for my journey toward scaling quickly and efficiently.

To Mikey Lucas, for opening my eyes to the many possibilities of tax-saving strategies. You have been my lighthouse in the storm, and I could not have navigated these challenging waters without you.

To my friends and family, you are my rock. Your support and encouragement have carried me through the late nights and early mornings that made this book possible. Your faith in me has been a motivating force like no other.

Last but certainly not least, I want to acknowledge my extraordinary team, 'The Dream 12'. Your constant grind and willingness to take what I give you and run with it inspire me to constantly improve so that I have more to give. You've not only helped me live my dream life but have also been instrumental in bringing this book to fruition. Your hard work and dedication make everything possible, and for that, I am endlessly grateful.

Thank you all for standing by me on this remarkable journey. This book is as much yours as it is mine.

With immense gratitude,

Michael Lanctot

Printed in the USA
CPSIA information can be obtained
at www.ICGtesting.com
LVHW061627030424
776154LV00020B/445